D1611015

THE LEGEND OF
EDDIE BAUER

BY ROBERT SPECTOR

THE LEGEND OF EDDIE BAUER

BY ROBERT SPECTOR

GREENWICH PUBLISHING GROUP, INC.
LYME, CONNECTICUT

Produced and published by Greenwich Publishing Group, Inc., Lyme, Connecticut

Design by Clare Cunningham Graphic Design Essex, Connecticut

Separation & film assembly by Silver Eagle Graphics, Inc.

Library of Congress Catalog Card Number: 94-77632

ISBN: 0-944641-06-7

First Printing: October 1994

10 9 8 7 6 5 4 3 2 1

Eddie Bauer

Eddie Bauer has become one of the world's most recognized brands. When Eddie first put his signature on products, it represented his personal pledge of satisfaction. Today, his signature symbolizes the company's commitment to the highest quality, value and service standards that Eddie established when he opened his first store in 1920.

A MAN WORTHY OF HIGH ESTEEM

A passion for the outdoors, an entrepreneur's dream and a few borrowed dollars. That's what Eddie Bauer started with when he opened his first store in Seattle in 1920, along with a reputation for sincere customer satisfaction.

It wasn't long after Eddie went into business for himself when he wrote Our Creed and Our Guarantee and implemented them with his customers. From that day forward, he stood staunchly behind those words without fail.

I admire the young man Eddie proved himself to be by these actions. In the tumultuous excitement of postwar America — when "get rich quick" schemes abounded — Eddie didn't set out to build an empire without regard for others; instead, he built a solid business by doing what's right. He cared about people...a rare quality then, even rarer today.

The 10,000-plus associates who comprise Eddie Bauer

OUR CREED
To give you such outstanding quality, value, service and guarantee that we may be worthy of your high esteem.

OUR GUARANTEE
Every item we sell will give you complete satisfaction or you may return it for a full refund.

today — the true owners of our business — are guided by Our Creed and Our Guarantee to deliver the same sincere service for which our founder was renowned.

I salute Eddie Bauer for his unquenchable spirit for life and adventure, his inventiveness and his optimistic vision of tomorrow's possibilities. I respect him for his integrity and the solid foundation of character he laid for this organization. I am grateful for this steadfast appreciation of people and for Our Creed and Our Guarantee. These words he so carefully wrote 75 years ago are still alive in our company today.

Eddie Bauer proved himself to be a man worthy of our highest esteem.

Rick Fersch

Rick Fersch, President

Ed learned the outdoors business at Piper & Taft, then Seattle's foremost sporting goods store, which carried gear for virtually every sport. In 1920, at the age of 20, Ed left P&T after seven years to open his own business, which would eventually dwarf that of Piper & Taft.

CHAPTER ONE

THE KID FROM ORCAS ISLAND

Eddie, please take care of this customer," boomed the voice of Archie Taft.

Responding immediately to his boss's order, 17-year-old Eddie Bauer stopped in the middle of stringing a tennis racket and hurried to the fishing department of the Piper & Taft sporting goods store to show a shopper the newest line of fishing tackle.

"When I worked, I never walked, I ran," Ed told a newspaper reporter more than six decades later. "Pretty soon, the customers were asking to have Eddie Bauer wait on them. Once your name has consumer and personal acceptance, you've got it made."

In the first three decades of the twentieth century, Piper & Taft was considered one of the best sporting goods retailers in the West. It filled six 7,500-square-foot floors with gear, clothing and footwear for virtually every sport, from fishing to football, and generated enough business to merit its own twice-a-year mail order catalog. Staffed by product experts, All-Americans, professionals and champions, Piper & Taft was a mecca for the Puget Sound region's hunters, trappers, fishermen, hikers, backpackers, campers and mountaineers.

Working at Piper & Taft was a dream job for young Ed, a lean and muscular six-foot-tall teenager. Long before he ever set foot in the store, virtually everything in Ed's life

and family background, "influenced me to become so keenly interested in hunting, fishing and outdoor activities and eventually prepared me for a successful career in outdoor outfitting," he wrote in his memoirs.

"I loved nature and learned to live off the land," he once said. "To me, having a good horse and a dog and running a trapline was the only way to live."

Ed was born October 19, 1899, on Orcas Island, in the San Juan Islands archipelago in Washington State's northern Puget Sound. An ideal starting place for a future sportsman, the region is blessed with a mild climate and an abundance of mountains, foothills, flatlands, valleys and assorted bodies of fresh and salt water, stretching 100 miles from the Cascade mountain range on the east to the Olympic mountain range on the west.

Ed was the last of six children born to Jacob and Mary Catherine Bauer, who were Russian immigrants of German ancestry. (Three of their first four children, who were born in Russia, had died in infancy.)

Ed's forefathers were late eighteenth-century Prussian mounted mercenaries who accompanied the German-born Empress Marie Catherine to Russia, where she married the heir to the Russian throne and later became known as Catherine the Great. They eventually became officers of the Cossacks — peasants who lived in communal

settlements and served in the czars' cavalry in exchange for property and special privileges. Ed's maternal grandfather was justice of the peace of Frank, a rich farming area near Russia's Volga River, and inherited a valuable concession of importing and training Arabian horses for the Cossacks. His paternal grandfather, governor of Frank, made hand-crafted boots for the cavalry. Each of Ed's grandparents had 13 children.

In 1890, Jacob and Mary Catherine decided to immigrate to America with their sole surviving child, Anna, who was then five years old. Their total assets (other than a few personal necessities) consisted of two Russian rubles, which were worth about one American dollar. Although he opposed

their decision, Grandpa Bauer assured Jacob and Mary Catherine that any time they wanted to return home, he would loan them the money to take care of their transportation expenses and any debts they might incur.

Jacob, Mary Catherine and young Anna arrived in Seattle a year after the Great Fire of 1889. The city was still rebuilding itself from the ruins of the fire, which destroyed virtually all of the 64-acre downtown core and left $10 million in damages. But rather than stunting the city's growth, the fire actually accelerated it. Population increased in the year after the disaster from 38,000 to 43,000. Many of the newcomers came to rebuild the city's unpaved streets and sewers

The Great Seattle Fire of 1889 destroyed virtually all of the young city's 64-acre downtown core and left $10 million in damages. The ships in the harbor were about all that escaped the conflagration. It was at this time, in 1890, when Ed's parents and his sister immigrated to Seattle from Russia.

Three decades after the Great Seattle Fire, the city had been rebuilt, and the bustling waterfront was an economic hub. This photograph was taken around 1920, the year that Eddie Bauer left Piper & Taft to open his own sporting goods shop. The building on the right is the Smith Tower, which was erected in 1914. At 42 stories, it was then the tallest building west of Chicago.

and erect new commercial buildings and schools. There were "enough brickmakers, masons, ironworkers, foundries, electrical workers, plumbers, cement manufacturers and roofers so that the fire was in fact a boon to an expanding and increasingly diversified economy," described historian Roger Sale in *Seattle Past to Present*. Others came to speculate on real estate, following the Great Northern Railroad's selection of Seattle (instead of arch-rival

Tacoma) as its terminus.

The tempo was feverish. Making money was on everyone's mind. A leading banker of that era described the mood as one "of adventure and wildcat speculation...such as can never again be witnessed." Norman H. Clark wrote in *Washington: A Bicentennial History*: "There had been nothing like it in the American history since the opening of the Louisiana Territory — golden years where no personal ambition, however

grandiose, seemed at all unreasonable, when it seemed that every venture might prosper and every family might share in the nobility of wealth because of the democracy of profit." But not everyone was so lucky. Yesler Way, a steep trail where timber workers skidded logs down the hill to Henry Yesler's steam sawmill on the waterfront, became the temporary home of vagrants, derelicts and other down-on-their-luck drifters. It was the source of the phrase that symbolized broken dreams, Skid Road. Today, Yesler remains a busy street ending on Seattle's waterfront.

Jacob and Mary Catherine had planned to find employment in Seattle long enough to raise money to homestead in eastern Washington, where they intended to farm wheat and other grains. Soon after their arrival, they were taken under the wing of Mr. and Mrs. Rolland H. Denny, members of a pioneering, influential Seattle family, who hired the Bauers as caretakers and gave them a homesite in what would eventually become the heart of the city — University Street and Fifth Avenue (a block from where the current Eddie Bauer flagship store now stands).

In 1897, gold had been found in the Klondike region of Canada's Yukon Territory. The discovery ignited the imagination of the world and made Seattle the gateway to the Klondike. That year, the Bauer family, which by then included their three-year-old daughter, Maria, sold their downtown property and moved to Orcas Island, where they lived in a small farmhouse at the end of the wagon road, which was the beginning of the trail up Mt. Constitution. The house was on an orchard property where Jacob Bauer grew Italian plums and kiln-dried them into prunes for commercial sales. Two years later, Ed was born. Life on picturesque Orcas Island was idyllic, and the wildlife was ideal for a future hunter and fisherman. The island teemed with a wide variety of game, including Columbia black-tailed deer, grouse, quail and cottontail rabbits. The

In 1897, gold was found in the Klondike region of Canada's Yukon Territory. The discovery ignited the imagination of the world and made Seattle the gateway to the Klondike; aspiring fortune-seekers clambered aboard any ship heading north. That year, the Bauer family sold their downtown property and moved to Orcas Island, in the San Juan Islands.

rich surrounding waters were home to king and silver salmon, halibut, flounder and sole, all varieties of cod and snapper and shellfish.

Although Ed's father didn't hunt or use firearms, he owned a shotgun and a rifle, which he made available to the young men on the island, who often stopped off at the Bauer place on the way up the mountain for deer and other game. Jacob skinned and butchered the game, cleaned the fish they caught and stocked these provisions in a screened cooling room that he built himself. Mary Catherine did the cooking.

At home, Jacob and Mary Catherine (whom everyone called Jake and Katie) always spoke German. Until he started attending school, Ed spoke only German. For the rest of his life, he spoke English to his parents, as did his sisters, but the parents' side of the conversation was always in German.

When Ed was five years old, his family moved to Yarrow Point, on the shores of Lake Washington, east of Seattle, where his father operated a dairy. It was here that the lad first learned how to fish with a rod for sport and "for the table." His father kept him well supplied with bait for fishing off a little dock. With this early experience, "I can well understand why all through my life I have been so keenly interested in fishing and fishermen."

He felt the same regard for the many hunters of upland birds who would stop for water — for themselves and their dogs — at the Bauer place, where Ed's mother supplied them with plums, apples and pears,

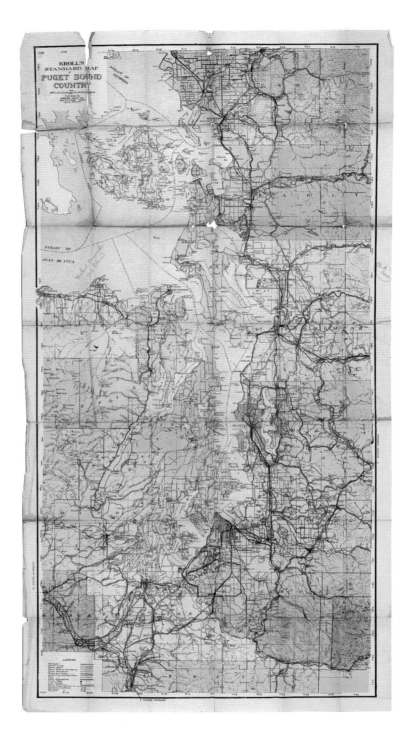

Ed was born on Orcas Island, the large, horse-shoe-shaped island to the west of Bellingham, at the top of this 1920 map. His family lived in a small farmhouse at the end of the wagon road, which was the beginning of the trail up Mt. Constitution. The house was on an orchard property where Jacob Bauer grew Italian plums and kiln-dried them into prunes for commercial sales. The island teemed with a wide variety of game and the rich surrounding waters were plentiful for fishing.

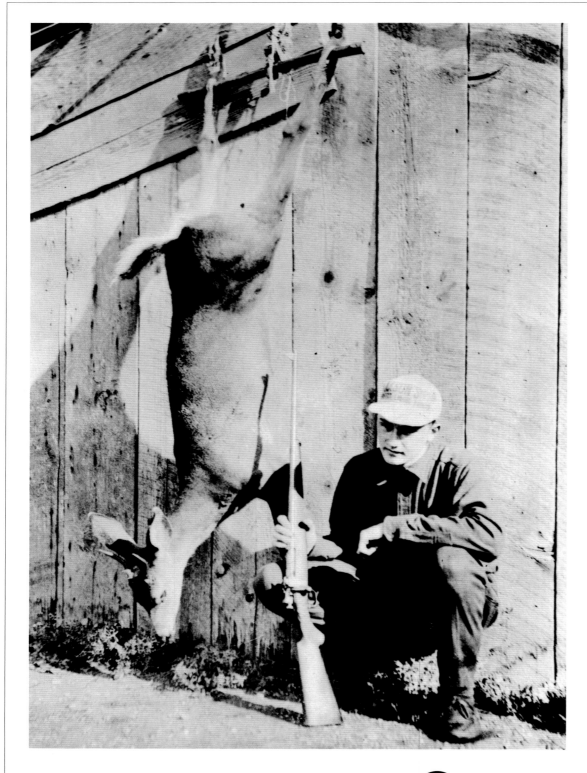

The Bauers, like many others at that time, lived off the land. Ed gained a respect for the environment as a place of beauty and a source of food. His passion for hunting and fishing intensified once he was exposed to the gear at Piper & Taft and the experts who sold it. By the time he took his first deer at the age of 15, he was already an accomplished outdoorsman. Ed's Excelsior motorcycle was a great joy, but the injuries sustained when he crashed into the back of a car cost him his job and caused medical problems later in life.

fresh off the tree. Ed watched closely the men who pursued quail, ruffed grouse and mallards and "dreamt of the day to come when I would be old enough to have a gun of my own and hunt for those beautiful birds."

His passion for hunting and fishing made Ed a self-described "black sheep" in the eyes of his cousins, whose interests ran to horses, farming, art, literature and classical music. "Yet everyone seemed to understand and appreciate the fact that I was different," he wrote. "At age five or six, I started clipping things I would buy some day out of mail order catalogs," from Sears and Montgomery Ward. "I had selected a saddle, bridle and spurs, also several firearms. I showed these to my father, who said, 'Some day, you will have those, no doubt.'"

When Ed was eight, his dad took him to the Ernst Hardware Store and bought him his first rifle — a Model 1890 Winchester .22 Special Caliber with an octagon barrel. Although it sounds hard to believe, Ed claimed in his memoir that he didn't fire the rifle with ammunition until three years later, when his family had moved to Bainbridge Island, across Elliott Bay from Seattle, where his father was caretaker of the Wing Point Golf and Country Club.

Around that time, Ed's Uncle Lesser arrived from Russia and came to stay with the family. Lesser regaled his young nephew with the tales of his exploits as a Cossack, particularly the time he had been wounded in bayonet combat in the Russo-Japanese War of 1904. "He had been run through from front to back with bayonets many times...through the arms, shoulders, neck and chest," recalled Ed, who saw the terrible scars for himself. "How he could survive was miraculous."

The Cossacks were able to endure the brutal cold in their forest encampments because their outer garments and fur headwear were interlined with quilted goose down. "I remember my dad saying that if it hadn't been for those down-lined coats the Cossacks wore, my uncle would have froze to death," Ed wrote. His uncle's experience piqued Ed's curiosity and "became very important to me in my business career and to my eventual use of goose down in the manufacture of down-insulated clothing and sleeping bags."

Ed's parents instilled in him a strong work ethic. At the age of 10, fueled by a desire to earn money to buy a double-barreled shotgun (a second-hand 16-gauge Fox Sterlingworth), he became a caddie at the Seattle Golf Club, where Uncle Lesser was caretaker and groundskeeper. His first caddying job was for Joshua Green, a legendary Seattleite who founded Peoples National Bank (which would later help finance many of Eddie Bauer's business operations). Ed soon agreed to do odd jobs at the Green residence; other club members wanted Ed to perform similar chores for them. He cut kindling and did a variety of errands in order to make money. This work "became a source of considerable revenue to me personally and I am sure inspired me to work and earn, and certainly these fine and prominent Seattleites and their families contributed ever so much good will towards building the Eddie Bauer business."

One of Ed's projects was to raise, winter-feed and eventually release in the wild Chinese pheasant hens for bird hunters. Caring for those pheasant "taught me that while I loved to hunt and take game and fish, that I should always like to contribute towards protection and propagation and felt it was my duty to always put back more than I took."

Even at the tender age of 10, outdoor activities weren't just Eddie Bauer's hobby, they were his life. His sixth-grade report card was "satisfactory, though I was excellent only in arithmetic and it is a wonder to me that I passed my grades because I was always daydreaming about the out of doors." A schoolgirl who had taken a fancy to him, laughingly asked Eddie if he did anything other than fish. "Sure," he answered. "I hunt."

A NEW LIFE

In 1913, Ed's life took a sudden turn when his mother and father told him they were separating. Offered the option of which parent to live with, he chose to go with his mother, who had gone through a series of illnesses and needed him more than Jacob did. Before departing for his new destination — his sister Anna's house in the Fremont neighborhood of Seattle — "I gathered my clothing and a few things that I had, took my rifle apart and wrapped it, and put a collar on my dog, Speed." He found his father and said good-bye. Suddenly, at the age of 14, Ed was the only

THE LEGEND OF EDDIE BAUER

man in the house. "It was a great misfortune, but I took it in stride."

Soon after arriving in Seattle, Ed found a part-time job to provide some much-needed cash for his mother. Piper & Taft needed a boy to work one hour in the morning before school, three hours after school until 6 p.m., and all day Saturday from 8 a.m. to 10 p.m. It seemed perfect for Ed. His initial duties included running errands, washing windows and doing other odd jobs around the store, for which he would be paid $18 a month. Needless to say, he was very excited about getting the job and hurried home to inform his mother. "I told her they couldn't have found a better place for me to work, that I just loved the sporting goods store...that I would work hard and make myself valuable to them. I knew no one would work harder than me. I also told my mother to start looking for a house of our own, that we could make it fine."

Although working at Piper & Taft was satisfying, it was also frustrating because school and work didn't leave Ed much time for fishing and hunting, "So, I decided something just had to be done about that and soon." The solution was provided by Piper & Taft's tackle manager, Sylvester Ellerby, who took a liking to the young man and gave Eddie a new rod and reel, an assortment of plugs and spinners and the use of a boat on Union Bay, an inlet of Seattle's Lake Washington.

Back in his natural element, Ed soon caught his first largemouth black bass and trout, which he proudly displayed on ice at the entrance of Piper & Taft. From then on,

many of Ed's catches were exhibited in displays assembled by Ed himself, who also lettered the cards that described the catches. "I soon became known as a pretty good fisherman. Quite frequently store customers would recognize me by saying, 'Hello, Eddie, how's fishing these days?' Many of them invited me to go with them to lakes and rivers beyond my reach via public transportation." His prowess in fishing (and later hunting) made Ed's name well known among Seattle's sports enthusiasts, and "I started feeling slightly more important than merely an errand boy." As the years went by, "the name of Eddie Bauer was given a great deal of publicity," which was "certainly a step forward in preparing me for my career. And for my employer, this publicity and news would certainly help bring many customers through the front door."

Ed gradually took on greater responsibilities. He became Piper & Taft's jack-of-all-trades, "spending all of my time in various departments, wherever the action was." He happily learned how to make fishing rods, gun stocks and custom golf clubs; and how to sell fishing tackle, footwear and outdoor apparel.

But that joyful time was turned upside down on the evening of May 8, 1917, when he was riding his beloved Excelsior motorcycle. "I was wild when I was young, like most boys," he recalled. "As I was riding up a steep hill, I lowered my head a bit and my hat covered my eyes. When I opened them, I was right on top of a Studebaker." The first impact came from the Studebaker's radiator. Ed fractured his

left leg and ankle, the left side of his jaw, and two vertebrae; his cheekbone was crushed.

It took him four months to recuperate to the point where he could return to work, but he was unable to work as hard as he had in the past. Because of the injury and slow sales at Piper & Taft, he was laid off in January 1918. But two months later — after working as a boilermaker and flue blower on a railroad locomotive — he was rehired, this time as manager of hunting and fishing clothing, camp goods, canoes and footwear. He was also put in charge of planning the store's publicity, advertising and window displays, giving him the opportunity to hone the promotional talents that he ultimately put to good use in the course of establishing the Eddie Bauer name. Ed's most noteworthy achievements came in the tennis department, where he oversaw racket-stringing operations. (In those days, all tennis racket frames were delivered unstrung.) "Ed was a big, strong, good-looking guy and Piper & Taft set him up stringing rackets in the front window of the store where everybody could see him," recalled Henry Allen, who worked with Ed at the store in 1919. "He strung those rackets tight."

Higher-priced rackets required lamb's gut string made by Armour and Company; lower-priced rackets (under $10 retail) used imported Japanese gut that cost about $.30 for a $2.50 or $3.00 restring job. "I put two and two together," recalled Ed, "and realized that stringing tennis rackets could be very profitable." In order to generate greater interest in tennis and promote his racket-stringing expertise, Ed purchased one of the best rackets that he had strung and — with his injured leg improved — spent a lot of time playing tennis at the Seattle public courts, where the rules allowed a player to remain on the court until he or she lost a match. Because Ed was good enough to occupy a court for a dozen or so sets, he came into contact with a steady procession of players and developed a clientele by convincing many of them to be his personal customers.

"All the people who played tennis found out about Eddie Bauer," said Henry Allen. "He had all the business in town, so when he opened his own store, he took all the customer names with him. He was no dummy."

In 1919, at the age of 18, Ed won a national contest for speed and proficiency in stringing tournament-caliber tennis rackets. He competed in the center window of Piper & Taft's 75-foot frontage on Second Avenue, where they set up a 20-foot-wide work area for a small racket-stringing bench and vice and a display of tennis equipment, clothing and footwear. For one full week, from 9 o'clock in the morning to 6 o'clock in the evening (with 30 minutes off for lunch) Ed — sportily dressed in white flannel tennis slacks, shirt and shoes — strung rackets at a pace of one finished racket every 13 to 15 minutes, which was an average of 24 every eight hours, "allowing 45 minutes of the eight hours away from the bench for personal needs," he remembered. Because Second Avenue was the busiest thoroughfare in the city, Ed's exploits

attracted hundreds of passersby. "I really put on a show for the folks and often there were opportunities to get the crowd laughing. The display proved to be a great success for the company and a great deal of personal publicity for me." Ed loved working at Piper & Taft, which was where he saw his future. "My hopes at that age were that I could become valuable to this fine company and be with them forever. I had not thought of ever personally going into business," he wrote. But things changed.

In 1920, with Piper & Taft going through a series of disruptive management changes, Ed made the decision to leave the store for good.

"It was with a heavy heart that I bid the Tafts and my friends farewell the last day of my employment on the day I would leave for a week of waterfowl shooting at the Skagit Flats."

His return would mark the beginning of a new era in the Seattle sporting goods business.

The vitality of Seattle's enterprising post–World War I business community is illustrated in this collection of advertisements on the curtain of a downtown theater. Soon, another name would be added to that collection: Bauer's Sport Shop.

While Ed's newly established Bauer's Sport Shop competed with his old employer, Piper & Taft, he maintained a friendly relationship with the owners of that fabled store. A believer in the power of public relations, Ed never passed up an opportunity to promote the Bauer name and his own prowess as a fisherman.

A BUSINESS OF HIS OWN

After leaving Piper & Taft, Ed spent the next year or so in a series of temporary jobs: sporting goods salesman during Christmas for the Frederick & Nelson department store, auto mechanic, real estate salesman and tire salesman. He was a good enough alto saxophone player to perform a few times with a local band. But, eventually, he felt "I should get back into the sporting goods business, the business I really loved."

This time, he would be on his own. He had completed a two-year business course and voraciously read Horatio Alger stories of men who achieved success with little formal schooling or personal wealth. With $25 in personal net worth, his goal was to make the name "Eddie Bauer" worth money. The combination of his well-publicized hunting and fishing exploits, winning personality, knowledge of the outdoors and popularity among Seattle sportsmen "made it possible for me to enter business without capital."

In 1920, Ed set up his own racket-stringing business, Eddie Bauer's Tennis Shop, in a small leased space at Bob Newton's Sporting Goods store, a block away from Piper & Taft, where for many years Newton had been the master gunsmith and rodmaker. Ed had enough money to buy a vice for stringing rackets, lumber to build a workbench, material for eight feet of shelving counters and a wall board to display rackets. Ed's father agreed to co-sign a $500 bank note to pay for his inventory of racket frames, gut strings and balls.

Archie Taft had once given Ed a piece of advice: "You can hire accountants, engineers, lawyers, advertising agencies, pros of all kinds. They are available by the thousands. The big secret to your success will be to get customers to come in that front door and spend their money." On that score, Ed didn't have a problem. "Fortunately," he wrote, "the customers came to me in large numbers. It seemed everyone was pulling for me, particularly the socially prominent Seattle families who had known my mother, father and me for so many years and were active in so many sports. Wherever the business came from, it came in a goodly amount and it allowed me to have a very substantial profit my first year."

Still, Ed didn't let business get in the way of his enduring love of the outdoors. Every year, right after Labor Day, he would put a sign over his work bench that said, "Eddie Bauer has gone hunting. Back February 1."

During his time off, Ed and his friends hunted and fished in every corner of the Pacific Northwest, from Oregon to British Columbia. He particularly relished his trips up the Elwha River on the Olympic Peninsula where he hunted upland birds and fished for steelhead trout. Also important were his excursions throughout eastern Washington (especially the Yakima Valley and the Okanogan Valley) to shoot upland birds, waterfowl, Chinese ring-necked pheasants, Hungarian partridge, blue grouse and deer. In his memoirs, he wrote about his love of the fishing on Dewatto Bay on Hood Canal, where "the shorelines and the Olympic mountains were spectacular.... The virgin forests were beautiful. Under them, as far as the eye could see, were rhododendrons in full bloom."

Henry Allen, who worked with Ed at Piper & Taft, recalled Ed as "a good guy in the woods and a helluva good hunting part-

STEELHEAD TROUT

Steelhead are sea-run rainbow trout. They are an anadromous species of fish that are born in fresh water, mature in the ocean and return to their birthplace to spawn. Both salmon and steelhead begin their journey home to the rivers where they were born after three to five years at sea. Today, these fish face many obstacles which contribute to their dwindling numbers. For instance, once in the river system, they must battle against dangerously low water levels from damming and the side-effects of the timber industry.

The salmon and steelhead runs in the Northwest no longer proliferate as they did in Eddie Bauer's youth. Still, rivers like the Lower Elwha and the Quinault on the Olympic Peninsula and the Skykomish and Stillaguamish which drain into the Puget Sound from the Cascades, remain productive areas for steelhead fishing in Washington today. The need to protect them remains constant. With the help of conservation programs that Bauer has supported, these rivers can continue to harbor steelhead and insure their existence.

ner. He liked to hunt and he knew how to hunt. He got to be a pretty good fisherman later on, but he was basically a hunter."

Eventually, Ed parted ways with Bob Newton and opened up his own tennis and golf store at 211 Seneca Street, a half-block from Newton's shop. Ed didn't have much money to fill the 200-square-foot space with inventory, so he employed a little fakery. To make people think he was carrying a wide variety of goods, he stocked his

shelves with dozens and dozens of empty shoe boxes, all with different labels. But when a customer pulled out a box and discovered it was empty, the secret was out. "This spread around among Seattleites like wildfire and it became a laughing matter with my customers when they came in to visit or make a purchase." The small size of the store did have one great advantage. "People walking by the window could see me either stringing tennis rackets or work-

Eddie Bauer's unconditional money-back guarantee gave Ed an opportunity to exhaustively test virtually each item sold in his store. The rod and reel that landed this huge king salmon in 1924 surely won Ed's admiration, and this photo might well have landed a few new customers. The fly, above, tied by Cam Sigler, Jr., is a pattern used for king salmon today.

ing on golf clubs. So, I did not have to do much advertising."

Ed expanded into fishing tackle and firearms. Henry Allen, who ran Piper & Taft's wholesale gun and fishing tackle departments, recalled how Eddie would outsmart his old bosses at Piper & Taft. His loyal customers, who preferred giving him their business, would first check out the selection of guns or fishing rods at Piper & Taft and then go tell Ed what model they wanted. "Eddie would leave them to watch his shop, and he would walk over to Piper & Taft and buy the item, wholesale, from

In the 1920s, Bauer's Sport Shop moved into this new, larger store on Seneca Street, which enabled Ed to broaden and increase his selection of goods for hunting, fishing, tennis and golf. While copies of the larger picture are in most Eddie Bauer stores today, few will recognize the original photo, right, with its many trophy deer. While demonstrating his skill was an important part of Ed's promotional strategy, the deer were air-brushed out of the picture in the 1970s as attitudes towards hunting changed.

me. Piper & Taft wasn't concerned about him because they didn't think he would ever amount to anything."

Ed's business prospered and Piper & Taft finally took him seriously. In his memoirs, Ed claimed that Piper & Taft tried to drive him out of the tennis racket business — his primary source of income — by under-selling every item that Ed carried by half the price. "I would never let them put me

out of business, even if I had to earn a living at some other type of work and operate the tennis shop as well," he wrote.

Luckily for Ed, the price war had the opposite effect. His friends rallied around him and the foot traffic in the store increased so much that he had to enlist the help of several lady friends (who were employed in other nearby businesses) to dust the shelves, mop the floor and wash

the windows. Every other day or so, Ed invited one of the ladies for dinner and to keep him company in the evening while he was stringing tennis rackets. "Often, wealthy people came to my place to pick out several high-priced rackets and would say to me, 'I do not actually need these new rackets, but I want to help make your business succeed in spite of...Piper & Taft.' My business did succeed, for I ended up with a

THE EDDIE BAUER CREED AND GUARANTEE

Eddie Bauer was built on a creed and a guarantee.

The creed: "To give you such outstanding quality, value, service and guarantee that we may be worthy of your high esteem."

The guarantee: "Every item we sell will give you complete satisfaction or you may return it for a full refund."

Ed placed the origin of his guarantee to the day "when my employer Archie Taft had told me that customer complaints should first go to the errand boy, then to one of the clerks, then to a department manager and then only as a last resort to any one of the Taft family who controlled the business. During my years with the firm I handled many customer complaints and I tried always to see the customer's point of view. In other words, the customer had to be satisfied at any cost," he recalled.

Ed had to relearn that lesson when he opened his own business. One day, a customer returned a tennis racket that had been purchased just a few days before. Ed had strung that racket "board tight," but it came back with the strings broken and expanded. The racket had obviously gotten wet. Ed agreed to restring the racket for cost, but told the customer that "no one could guarantee high quality lamb's gut tennis strings" on a racket that had been left out in the rain.

But the customer insisted that no such thing had happened, that the strings had just gone bad on their own.

"With that remark, I really blew my top and told him so," Ed recalled. "I went to work stringing tennis rackets and left him standing there to think it over. I, too, did a bit of thinking. Customers came and left, and all the while this fellow, whose name was Jack, stayed there and said nothing. Finally, I realized this whole situation was comical so I started laughing out loud. I said, 'Jack, I'm going to string your racket and I'll do a good job. The customer is always right.'

"Jack was receptive and I did a beautiful tournament stringing job for him, gave it to him and asked him to please not let it get wet. He thanked me and I think from then on, he could not help but have a good word for me. He did me a great favor, because he helped me establish a guarantee and a creed."

Following a dispute over stringing a racket similar to this, Ed initiated a guarantee that is still in effect today.

Bill Lindbergh, Bauer's in-store fishing expert, had been Ed's fishing companion since childhood. In the 1920s, the two old friends saw a new market in local saltwater fishing. The first to promote saltwater salmon fishing in the Northwest, they added a new dimension to sportfishing and created a new industry.

The company backed its promotion of salmon spinning with a series of ads in the *Seattle Times*. The salmon in the cans below was caught by Eddie and distributed to his friends and associates. The camaraderie that motivated these gifts is an enduring part of the Eddie Bauer culture.

profitable season and, as a result of the half-price sale, I had been given a huge amount of good will by the people of Seattle."

In the late 1920s, Ed moved into a new and larger store at 223 Seneca Street, which enabled him to increase his product inventories for hunting, fishing, tennis and golf and to diversify into squash and badminton. (He was personally active in all of those sports, particularly rifle shooting, pistol shooting and trapshooting, where he was a tournament-caliber competitor.) He expanded his assortment of locally produced fishing tackle and coined the snappy advertising slogan, "Foxy tackle for frisky fish." He also added outdoor clothing and eiderdown sleeping bags. (Eider is the name for any of several large sea ducks that live in northern regions of Europe, Asia and North America.) As Seattle's newly crowned headquarters for hunting and fishing, "we were the best informed and made it a point to be thoroughly reliable in our outfitting and all information we handed out." The importance of being knowledgeable about sports and equipment and clothing would be a hallmark of the Eddie Bauer organization.

Ed prided himself on catering to a vast cross-section of customers. People "were all the same to us and whether they were wealthy with world famous titles or the most humble they were all treated exactly the same and all would receive the same welcome and the same warm, cordial, personal service. The wealthiest Seattleites including businessmen, bankers, professional men traded with us, as did the police, sher-

iffs and federal law enforcement people. Often these people would meet (always cordially) well-known rumrunners, moonshiners and bootleggers. Indians from many of the reservations came to our place to make purchases, and I often hunted and fished with them."

Ed always believed that an important way of building business was to promote new outdoor activities. One example was salmon saltwater sportfishing. At the time, western Washington fishermen considered salmon a food fish (in a class with cod and halibut), while sportfishing was limited to fresh water. To change that perception, Ed capitalized on advice that Archie Taft had given him a few years before: The Pacific Northwest "was sleeping at the switch, that there was a terrific volume of tackle sold for ocean fishing in California and along the Atlantic Coast. He suggested I concentrate on the saltwater fishing for sport."

In a 1927 direct mail letter to his customers, Ed wrote that Bill Lindbergh, his in-store fishing expert and a fishing companion since childhood, "has fished every lake, river and stream in western Washington and spent a year in Alaska trolling for salmon. He took salmon on light spinning tackle and caught sea-run cutthroat when few fishermen in the Northwest realized there was such sport in saltwater fishing in our locality." Ed and Lindbergh formed a club, called the Sockos. "When we fished, we'd anchor perhaps fifty to a hundred yards apart and we would be strung out perhaps a half mile or so in length," Ed recalled. "Whenever anyone

STINE BAUER

*I*n the late 1920s, Ed met Christine Heltborg on a grouse-hunting trip with friends at Bodie Mountain in eastern Washington. Christine, whom everyone called "Stine," was just as personable as she was attractive and independent (she operated her own Seattle beauty shop). On camping trips, she was "the life of the party," Ed recalled. "She sang and played the ukulele and entertained all of us." Stine made a lasting impression on Ed on one cold, blustery spring day when both were part of a group that was braving inclement weather on a day trip. "There was rain, sleet mixed with snow, and it was unusual to me that a girl would so enjoy a rugged outing of that kind."

In the early 1920s, Ed had been engaged briefly to one woman and was later married for a short time to another. Neither woman was as interested in the outdoors as Stine, "who took to fishing, camping, hiking, boating and trapshooting as enthusiastically and as well as the men who had been my companions. Once she was shown how to dress out a buck, she did not hesitate doing her own. She had far greater stamina than I did."

While they were dating, Stine and Ed often went to the Seattle Gun Club where Ed was a member of the club's top five-man trapshooting team. "She was an attractive girl and the men at the gun club gave her much of their attention," Ed recalled. "Often they tried to show her the proper stance and teach her how to shoot

clay pigeons. One day Stine said to me, 'Why don't you ever try to show me about trap shooting?' I answered that she had never asked me to and that...you could never learn to shoot by trying to take instructions from a number of people. I told her I would be glad to teach her how to break clay birds, but she would have to listen to my advice and instructions and take no heed of what others might tell her. She said, 'let's do that.'"

Stine and Ed were married on February 21, 1929, and stayed together the rest of their lives. He affectionately called her "my wilderness companion."

In a 1940 interview with the Seattle *Post-Intelligencer*, Stine was asked if she was ever sorry she married Eddie. She replied: "No, indeed, not yet anyway! We have so many things in common. We both enjoy trapshooting, skiing, mountain climbing, fishing and other sports."

Stine Bauer, above and right, rowing her friend Virginia Denny and Mrs. Denny's mother, was a radiant woman who represented the heart of the Eddie Bauer company. Stine was an accomplished sports–woman who was as adept as her husband with rifle or fishing rod. She and Ed were married for 56 years.

Emil Johnson, Eddie, Stine and Gotch Coho with their catch, circa 1928. Ed once wrote that Stine "took to fishing, camping, hiking, boating and trapshooting as enthusiastically and as well as the men who had been my companions."

ED AND STINE — SHOOTING CHAMPIONS

*E*d was one of the finest all-around shots in the country, whether it was with a pistol, a rifle or a shotgun," recalled Ted Van Theil, who managed the fishing tackle and gun departments for Ed from 1931 through 1939. "I remember one time someone was mouthing off about hitting a 36-inch bull's-eye at 600 yards and someone else said it couldn't be done. Ed said, Hell, he could do it with a couple of practice shots. We got 25 bucks up and he went out and shot 21 bull's-eyes in a row until it got too dark to shoot. He proved his point. Whatever he did, he was very good at it."

Ed and Stine were trapshooting champions, separately and as a team. From 1930 to 1937, Stine held the Washington State women's trapshooting championship as well as numerous other regional titles. In 1932, Ed won the Class AA championship in the Washington State Trapshooting Association's meet, hitting 192 clay pigeons out of 200. He won many side bets for himself and for spectators who put their money on him. "I am somewhat proud of the fact that I never disappointed those who had confidence in me," he wrote. That same year, in what the *Seattle Times* called "probably the finest bit of husband-and-wife trapshooting in the history of the sport," Ed broke 99 clay pigeons out of 100 and Stine broke 94 to win the Seattle Gun Club's "Papa and Mamma" trophy at Fort Lawton.

"Because of our performance, Stine and I were able to get a great deal of beneficial publicity for the Eddie Bauer business," Ed recalled. For example, around Thanksgiving 1932, the Seattle *Post-Intelligencer* published a picture of Ed posing with four 280-pound bucks (two of them shot by Stine) on a six-week hunting trip to British Columbia. "Stine and I continued attending practically all of the shoots until shortly before our son, Eddie Christian Bauer, was born, February 5, 1938. I then carefully cleaned and oiled our trap guns and put them away in their cases where they remained for 20 years."

From 1930 to 1937, Stine held the Washington State women's trapshooting championship and many other regional titles. The photo, right, catches Stine posing in the field for a newspaper photographer. Ed, far right, modeled his classic Stetson, Pendleton shirt and Parker shotgun about 1926.

hooked a fish they would stand up to play it and loudly shout the word 'socko' — meaning 'I have a strike'." The word also informed everyone down the line of the presence of a school of fish. "Once everyone was into the school, no one shouted 'socko' unless they happened to hit a big one."

Charles Lindaman, one of Ed's Socko friends, was an advertising manager for the *Seattle Times*. He prepared a full-page article on salmon fishing in the *Times*, with a picture of Lindbergh and Christine Heltborg (the future Mrs. Eddie Bauer) standing beside Ed's boat with a fine catch of salmon. "Charley's article really set the sport fishing in motion and it just grew by leaps and bounds from that day on," Ed recalled.

Here's another example of Ed's mastery of self-promotion — a quote in a supposed-ly objective article about Ed in the *Seattle Times*: "Come one, come all," says Eddie. "We'll give them just what they need for fishing, golfing, tennis-playing, riding, hiking and whatever sport they intend featuring during their vacation. And if there's any special dope we can give about where to go for this or where to go for that to make the vacation just a little pleasanter, you can bet we'll gladly give it!"

Despite the 1929 stock market crash and the ensuing years of depression, which brought about the failure of many retailers, Eddie Bauer's sales and profits grew every year. While sales of the most costly mer-chandise declined, the popular-priced necessities increased greatly. How did Bauer

Because Ed and Stine were frequently on skis, it was easy for him to understand the potential for skiing as a recreational sport. In the 1930s, he began importing hickory skis from Norway. Ed later bankrolled ski champions Olaf Ulland of Norway and Scott Osborn of Seattle in the Osborn & Ulland sporting goods shop, which continues in business to this day.

buck the trend? Ed's customers — from tradesmen to bankers — told him that they had worked hard and long for many years, "so since they weren't busy at the time, they figured they might as well catch up on a bit of recreation," he recalled.

Ed continued to move to larger stores on the same block of Second Avenue and Seneca Street. In 1934, with the financial backing of an older friend, Dan Smith, he moved into a 6,600-square-foot space and added imported hickory skis from Norway. (In order to promote the skiing business in the Pacific Northwest, the Norwegian government would send over their top skiers, who worked in sporting goods stores in the region. Ed later bankrolled Olaf Ulland, one of the visiting Norwegian ski champions, and Seattle ski champion Scott Osborn in the Osborn & Ulland sporting goods shop, in which he kept a 50 percent ownership. Osborn & Ulland is still in business today.)

He also added special customized goods departments, such as Eddie Bauer Tackle Makers and Eddie Bauer Shuttle Makers for badminton shuttlecocks. The interior of the store was decorated with mounts of Ed's game trophies, wildlife paintings and enlarged photographs of famous mountain climbers and ski scenes. Ed's wife, Stine, whom he had married in 1929, was in charge of all of the women's sports apparel.

The entire 60-foot width of the back of the store was subleased to Ome Daiber's Hike Shack, which stocked mountain-climbing equipment such as backpacks, rucksacks, tents and packboards. At the

WE WILL PAY $1.00 TO ANYONE MAKING A CASH PURCHASE IN THIS STORE WHO IS NOT TENDERED A PRINTED REGISTER RECEIPT, SHOWING CORRECT AMOUNT OF PURCHASE. CLAIM TO BE MADE BEFORE LEAVING STORE.

BAUERS

IMPORTERS, MANUFACTURERS AND DISTRIBUTORS OF

GOODS

"HOBBY HEADQUARTERS"
Where All Sportsmen Meet

Badminton . . . Squash . . . Golf . . . Sports Apparel
Camper's Needs . . . Outing Supplies . . . Hunting
and Fishing Equipment . . . Tennis Supplies

EDDIE BAUER
Who Trades as Bauer's Sporting Goods
Second at Seneca   SEATTLE   SEneca { 2525
                                            { 2526
We Will Not Be Undersold

In 1938, Ed moved his retail operations to a larger store in the Washington Athletic Club. The flyer, left, states Ed's policy of always providing a sales receipt; small items like laces, lures and hooks might have been given to a customer in an envelope such as the one shown here.

BADMINTON

During the depression years, badminton became widely popular throughout Canada and Europe, but less so in the United States, perhaps because of a 60 percent tariff on imported shuttlecocks. To help promote the game locally, Ed traveled to Canada and purchased at wholesale large quantities of tournament-weight shuttlecocks. Soon, local badminton enthusiasts (mostly tennis players) rented a building with enough room for two badminton courts.

But the players complained that the shuttlecocks (which were supposed to weigh 87 grains — almost 0.2 of an ounce) were widely inconsistent in weight — varying by as much as 15 grains from the lightest to the heaviest — and consequently, widely inconsistent in the distance they traveled when struck.

Believing that a high-quality shuttlecock would find willing buyers, Ed set out to make the best shuttlecock money could buy. He used goose quills (which he got from one of his fishing tackle suppliers), specially manufactured cork and the best kidskin. To make them all one standard weight, Ed filled the shuttlecocks with bird shot, which was readily available and easy to handle. "I had weighed all of the sizes of shot carefully on a jeweler's scale and found that I could vary a counterbalancing weight by one grain," he recalled.

Ed and a local die maker designed a piece of equipment that held a shuttlecock in a firmly secured upside-down position. A

hole was pierced in the cork base. Then bird shot was inserted into the base until each shuttlecock was the same weight, which gave it greater consistency in flight than any other on the market.

In 1934, Ed secured U.S. and Canadian patents on the Bauer shuttlecock, which greatly revolutionized the industry throughout the world and enabled the game to become popular throughout the United States, where his shuttlecock was adopted for national tournaments.

Unfortunately, Ed was forced to stop production during World War II when quality goose down was no longer available from central Europe. At the same time, Japan blocked the shipment of quality down from China.

When Ed couldn't find quality products from existing manufacturers, he didn't hesitate to create his own. The uniform weight of his badminton shuttlecock gave it greater consistency in flight than any other on the market. His company, Bauer's Shuttles, Inc., produced his patented shuttlecocks, which were the best money could buy.

time, Ome Daiber was the Pacific Northwest's premier mountaineer (in the 1920s, he had led the first ascent on the north wall of Mt. Rainier). He was also a noted skier, Yukon expeditioner and designer of outdoor products, including the form-fitting Penguin sleeping bag, which had arms and legs.

THE DAWN OF THE DOWN REVOLUTION

Ed's customers knew that Ed himself had personally subjected every style of equipment he sold to a rugged field test — a corporate philosophy that continues to this day. "If I didn't trust a piece of equipment, it wasn't stocked," he said. Instead, he'd often craft a new and improved version. "If I needed equipment that wasn't available elsewhere, I developed it myself. That's what led to my invention of quilted goose down clothing."

Ed was aware of the benefits of down from the stories of his Cossack uncle in the Russo-Japanese War, as well as his own firsthand experience. On one particular fishing trip on the Olympic Peninsula, Ed was caught in a freezing rain; his soaked clothing and his backpack (which was loaded with freshly caught steelhead) quickly became covered with ice. Ed started to feel drowsy, as if he were about to fall asleep. He then fired three shots in the air to signal his fishing partner, who had gone on ahead. "I sat down with my back against a tree and was dozing off when my fishing partner came along and shook me awake. I

was suffering from what we now know is hypothermia, and I'd have been a goner if my partner hadn't come along."

In 1935, Ed decided to manufacture a warm, lightweight jacket, made from goose down, for skiers and mountaineers who braved the snow and glaciers of the Pacific Northwest and Alaska. Most of the outdoor apparel available at that time — woolen pants, woolen underwear, Mackinaw coats — were heavy, particularly when wet. Goose down, Ed knew, offered three important benefits: it held just the right amount of air to retain all body warmth; it stopped the penetration of outside cold and moisture; and it allowed free circulation of air throughout the down to prevent dampness. Down "breathes," which means that it wicks body moisture to the outer surface of the garment, where it evaporates. This precludes the garment getting soggy, heavy and uncomfortable.

His first effort to design down outerwear created not just a jacket, but a revolution, with a garment that featured distinctive visible diamond quilting to hold the down in place. At the time, Ed claimed that there had never been a visibly quilted outdoor apparel garment manufactured and sold in the United States, although there might have been garments interlined with machine quilting. (The Chinese had been hand-quilting clothing for ages.) He cut a pattern, had a seamstress make a sample, and then showed it to Ome Daiber, who "put the jacket on, closed it, tested it for freedom of movement and he was a happy young man," Ed recalled. Daiber agreed to

manufacture the jacket exclusively for Eddie Bauer, who financed the production and imported the raw northern waterfowl down through a separate Eddie Bauer company called Arctic Feather & Down Co.

A small ad in *Field & Stream*, the national hunting and fishing magazine, generated hundreds of orders for what was then called the Eddie Bauer Blizzard-Proof® jacket. The garment was made out of unbleached muslin sheeting (which was dyed forest green). It had knitted, alpaca-lined sleeves. The Blizzard-Proof® jacket was succeeded by an improved version called the Skyliner®, which became a big seller. The next fall, Ed designed the Yukon® model, which had square, quilted down-filled pouches. Both the Skyliner® and the Yukon®, which became perennial favorites, could keep the wearer warm at temperatures well below zero.

After receiving design patents on the Skyliner® and the Yukon® in 1936, Ed then designed "every imaginable type of quilting — square, vertical and herringbone — and style of garment for both men and women." He was eventually awarded 16 different U.S. design patents for quilted clothing. "With this patent protection, I had virtually a monopoly on the entire quilted clothing business for the U.S. until approximately 1952," he recalled. "Others couldn't compete with me [on price] because we manufactured our own products and sold direct to the customer."

He wrote to the United States Weather Bureau and "asked them to inform me of the coldest regions in the world that were

After he almost froze to death in the woods, Ed saw an opportunity to make clothing that would keep people warm in extreme conditions. The result was the famous Eddie Bauer Blizzard-Proof® parka and the creation of another new industry. Ed held many patents for quilted clothing. This advertisement, right, appeared in the *Seattle Times* on July 26, 1942.

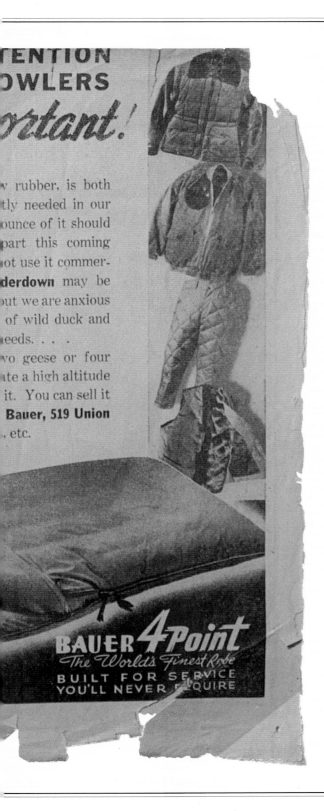

DOWN

*D*own is one of the miracles of nature. The basic elements of down's remarkable insulating capacity are hundreds of microscopic feelers radiating from the center of a down cluster. These feelers have innumerable hairs, each of which serve as an agent of insulation.

Because down is porous, it "breathes," which means it lifts body moisture — which is superior to air for conducting heat — to the outer surface of the garment, where it evaporates. Evaporation prevents the garment from getting soggy, heavy and uncomfortable. As a natural insulator, down retains body warmth and resists the penetration of outside cold and moisture and allows free circulation of air, which also serves to prevent dampness.

Among all insulating materials, down has the greatest capacity to retard heat loss because of its high level of loft — volumetric measurement by weight. The greater the loft, the greater the thermal efficiency. Down also outperforms all other insulating materials in its ability to sustain loft over the life of the garment.

Eddie Bauer understood these qualities, which is why he made down insulation the heart of the Eddie Bauer product line.

Ed wrote much of his own advertising and coined memorable slogans like "foxy tackle for frisky fish" and "what's up with down." Ed's ad, right, was part of a Christmas promotion for down clothing.

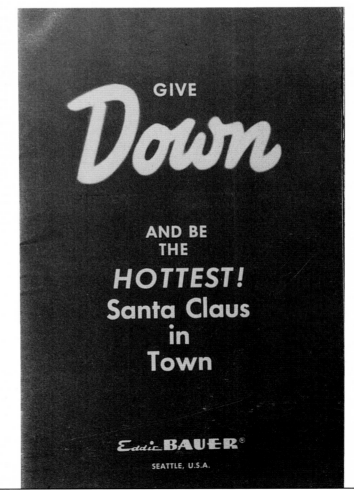

SLEEPING BAG PRODUCTION
THE EDDIE BAUER WAY

Civilian and military-issue Bauer sleeping bags were the warmest money could buy. Some soldiers in Alaska reportedly bartered their highly regarded bags in poker games.

To produce sleeping bags more efficiently for the war effort, Ed devised a new production method. Under the old method, after the fabric was cut for the sleeping bag, two men used a straight edge and chalk to mark where the seams would be sewed. This procedure was costly and time-consuming, so Ed devised a machine that automatically ruled the fabric and conveyed it to long tables where it was cut to size.

He also designed a device that permitted one sewing machine to completely assemble all of the sleeping bags' zippers and webbing at the same time. And to package the finished product, he fashioned an apparatus that would grasp one end of the sleeping

bag and roll it so tightly that it could fit into a storage bag that was 70 percent smaller in size than competitors' bags.

"The inspection officers that were sent in to keep an eye on our production kept this secret. By doing so it placed us in a position to underbid anyone else in the industry. We were able, or would have been, to make all the sleeping bags required for the Armed Forces," Ed recalled.

Later, to cooperate with the war effort, he prepared a brochure for his competitors that detailed these methods.

inhabited by people," he wrote in his memoirs. "In doing this, I really had in mind selecting names for my garments and sleeping bags that were insulated for extreme cold." In addition to Yukon®, those names included Polar King® and Kara Koram® (a different spelling of Karakoram, the mountain range in northern Kashmir and Pakistan).

Even before Ed received his patent on the Skyliner®, Father Hubbard, who was famous at the time as the "glacier priest" of the Arctic, relied on the jacket exclusively for his mercy missions and scientific explorations in the North Pole region. Soon, the Skyliner® was also chosen by Sir Hubert Wilkins and Alaska bush pilot Joe Crosson for their flying expeditions in the Arctic and Antarctic. The exploits of these adventurers gave the garment widespread publicity, prompting other Alaska bush pilots, such as Carl Ben Eielson and Bob Reeve, to start wearing the jacket, which was a vast improvement over the heavy fur Eskimo parkas they had been wearing.

With the popularity of the goose-down garments, as well as several styles of goose-down insulated sleeping bags, Ed launched the Eddie Bauer Expedition Outfitters mail order division, which enabled him to bypass the middlemen in the retail distribution process and maintain the retail price of the items despite rising costs of down. (Mail order sales were generated by magazine advertising. Bauer did not issue a catalog until the end of World War II.) Eventually, Ed took over production from Ome Daiber, who was not set up to meet the growing demand. "I started with 10 seamstresses and eventually had 125 seam-stresses," Ed told *Pacific Northwest* magazine in 1983. In 1938, Ed moved his retail oper-ations to a larger store on Sixth Avenue and Union Street in the Washington Athletic Club Building, which was the meeting center of sporting activity in Seattle. He personally managed the store until 1941, when the United States' entry into World War II steered his life in another direction, one which had a momentous impact on his fiscal and physical health.

Perhaps more than anything else, this label was responsible for the company's rapid postwar growth, as returning military people created a demand for Eddie Bauer products in every corner of America.

WAR PRODUCTION

In early 1942, the U.S. Army needed Eddie Bauer's help. A Japanese submarine had destroyed several U.S. cargo vessels en route from Seattle to Alaska. Their cargoes included sleeping bags for troops stationed in Alaska. The Quartermaster Corps asked Ed to purchase for them every available cold-weather sleeping bag, snowshoe and snowshoe harness in the entire United States and Canada. Ed telephoned every source he knew of — including some famous competitors — and had them immediately ship the equipment to Bauer headquarters.

Bauer worked with Ducks Unlimited to publicize to American sportsmen the urgent need for every possible ounce of waterfowl feathers and down for war production, which was called the Gathering Campaign. "It would have been impossible for any small operator to purchase the many, many thousands of dollars of space that was given to advertising this effort. The goodwill that came from this was priceless. It was of great benefit and advertising value for the years to come."

To produce sleeping bags for the army, the War Production Board (WPB) requisitioned and purchased Bauer's vast quantity of fabrics, zippers, snaps and high-quality goose down and put a production freeze order on Arctic Feather & Down Co. and Eddie Bauer Expedition Outfitters. Ed's only consolation was that "the Quartermaster gave me a written agreement that regardless of the freeze order on fabrics, all of this material would be replaced to me as soon as I required it."

As Eddie Bauer Expedition Outfitters became an important supplier to the army, Ed was faced with a balancing act: patriotically producing goods for the war effort while still maintaining some portion of his civilian production of clothing and sleeping bags. The scales were tipped to war production when the WPB ordered a freeze on the sale of all domestic duck and goose down, thereby bringing a virtual halt to civilian output. Ed reacted by buying huge quantities of eiderdown, the next best substitute for goose down. (Eider is as efficient as goose in terms of thermal insulation, but it tends to clump together and can't easily be blown into place during the manufacturing process.) While approving Bauer's consumer production of eiderdown-insulated clothing, the WPB restricted sales to veterinarians, doctors, ranchers, construction workers and other occupations exposed to the cold. Customers who sent in orders were required to fill out an application card to verify their need for the protective clothing.

Because of the shortage of waterfowl feathers and down for war production, Ed developed a substitute material out of small, curled chicken feathers, which were available in great quantities throughout the United States. The United States Army's Materiel Lab at Wright Field in Dayton, Ohio, tested the chicken feathers and found them suitable for sleeping bags for all of the armed forces. Ed went to Dayton to help write the specifications for this insulating material, and soon large purchase orders were issued to Ed and several other manufacturers. Then the trouble began. Major John Schenk, the acting commander of the Materiel Lab, telephoned Ed and told him that the sleeping bag manufacturers felt that Ed's specifications for the feathers' cleanliness were impossible to achieve, as was the required volume of production. Ed told Schenk that he would personally guarantee production and delivery of all the sleeping bags needed if the army made sure he was given priority in purchasing the necessary equipment. "I informed [Major Schenk] I'd probably go broke complying, because of the investment required, but I would nevertheless do it for the war effort."

Ed got the priority and swung into action. He purchased a four-story, wood-frame building in Seattle for the Arctic Feather & Down operation and bought the large and complex feather-processing equipment. He also formed a subsidiary called Feathers, Inc., which made Feather Foam, a down-like substance from chicken feathers. Ed owned Feathers, Inc., outright. To finance the $75,000 investment, he had to give the bank his personal guarantee, "so the risk was all mine and I knew it," he recalled. Out of that one building, Eddie Bauer supplied the army with down substitutes. At its peak, the company was cleaning and drying 14,000 pounds of curled chicken feathers every day.

Arctic Feather & Down produced and delivered 1,000 sleeping bags within the first 60 days of operation. "We were informed that other contractors were so far

In the early 1950s, Eddie Bauer Alaska Outfitters was located on Jackson Street in Seattle, where Bauer manufactured its products and conducted its fledgling mail order business. The initial mailing list consisted of several shoe boxes containing 14,000 names — almost all of them military men who had become Eddie Bauer aficionados during the war when they learned they could depend on their Bauer clothing and sleeping bags.

delinquent that we could manufacture a second thousand at once. This we did without any problem," Ed recalled. Arctic Feather & Down then plunged into 24-hour-a-day production of sleeping bags, employing over 400 people in three eight-hour shifts, producing 120,000 units in one year. Most of these sleeping bags were used by soldiers in the "thousand-mile war," the Aleutian campaign that followed the Japanese invasion of the islands of Attu and Kiska in June 1942.

At virtually the same time, the WPB ordered 10,000 packboards — for the mountain troops — to be ready for ship-

ment in two days. Arctic Feather & Down did all the canvas and leather work for the packboards, which were produced and assembled at the Osborn & Ulland sport shop. "The smoothness with which this assembly and delivery took place in this two-day period was phenomenal," Ed recalled. "It attracted crowds by the thousands to watch the vans delivering components and hauling away the crated finished products."

For the first few years of the war, Ed had been unofficially supplying flying suits (parkas and pants) to officers stationed at Sand Point Naval Air Station in Seattle and Elmendorf and Ladd fields in Alaska. The officers loved the flying suits so much that they paid for them out of their own pockets. Pilots, copilots, navigators, bombardiers, gunners and other flight-crew members flew their long missions in drafty, virtually unheated aircraft. The warmth of the down clothing gave them not only much-needed comfort but significantly increased their productivity and ability to perform their missions successfully. The efficiency of the down-insulated flight suits was such that a person could withstand temperatures as low as 70 degrees below zero for three hours. Another important feature was buoyancy: the triangular quilting that held down in place also trapped air. It was said that an Eddie Bauer flight suit could keep a downed airman afloat for up to 24 hours.

Major Schenk, at the army's Materiel Lab, had heard about these marvelous flying suits and arranged a meeting with Ed in order to procure them for the air corps. After the meeting, Ed agreed to supply the badly needed flying suits, one of which is on display at the Museum of History & Industry in Seattle. "Because of the quality of our products, countless lives were saved from drowning, hypothermia, exhaustion and other unforeseen disasters," Ed proudly recalled.

The reliable performance of Eddie Bauer jackets and sleeping bags made them famous among military personnel, whose word-of-mouth endorsements were, Ed believed, "the best advertising of all." It also helped that Ed was able to talk the military into letting him sew the Eddie Bauer label into each garment. It was the only private manufacturer's label to appear on government-issue gear during the war.

The importance of Ed insisting that his label be sewn into the flight suits would not be felt for years, but it probably was the single most important factor that fueled the company's growth. The prewar Eddie Bauer name was known only to sportsmen in the Pacific Northwest and to a handful of others whom the store outfitted for exotic expeditions. The returning aviators, however, scattered to their hometowns in every part of America taking with them the sure knowledge that Eddie Bauer clothing provided superior comfort under the most adverse conditions. As swashbuckling heroes, held in high esteem by those around them, the aviators spread the Eddie Bauer name further and more effectively than would otherwise have been possible. One day, these customers would become the nucleus of Eddie Bauer's multimillion dollar mail order business.

EDDIE'S HEALTH

Ed's increased responsibilities, financial obligations and long hours on the job were taking their toll. With his young managers, Osborn and Ulland, in the armed forces, Ed shouldered the burden of three corporations involved in war production — Arctic Feather & Down; Feathers, Inc., and Eddie Bauer Expedition Outfitters. The strain of acquiring raw materials during the war years, managing the myriad of manufacturing operations and meeting demanding delivery schedules put an increasingly heavy burden on Ed. He set the operating strategies and successfully managed most of the business, but the details often overwhelmed him.

Frequent severe backaches were sometimes "almost unbearable," he recalled; one episode kept him in bed for a week. Spinal x-rays taken during a physical examination revealed that at some point in his life he had suffered a double spinal fracture. (He surmised that it might have been from his motorcycle crash in the summer of 1918.) Medication relieved the pain and saw him through this stressful period.

Another source of stress was Ed's personal and corporate financial condition. In 1946, Eddie Bauer, Inc., the retail store, was losing money and Ed was relying on bank credit to keep his business operations going. Ed owned all of the common stock in Eddie Bauer, Inc.; the preferred stock was owned largely by Sarah Jane Smith, who was the widow of Dan Smith, the Seattle businessman who helped finance the business in 1934. After Smith passed away, Ed looked for a way to buy her shares and get both of them out of the retail business. He found a buyer for the store who was willing to let Ed retain possession of the Eddie Bauer corporate name. But Mrs. Smith decided not to sell.

Aware that Ed was in poor health, she appointed a man named Carl Nue as manager to take over Ed's operational duties, but Ed was insistent on making his life less complicated and taking it in a different direction.

In 1947, he sold his 50 percent interest

in two local sporting goods stores that he had initially bankrolled, Bill Lohrer, Inc., and Osborn & Ulland. He wanted to raise as much capital as he could so that he could accumulate real estate in Bellevue and other choice property in the rapidly developing Seattle suburbs east of Lake Washington. To achieve that end, he persisted in the desire to liquidate the inventory and assets of the retail store, Feathers, Inc., and Arctic Feather & Down (leaving him with Eddie Bauer Expedition Outfitters, the manufacturing and mail order business).

Ed claimed in his memoir that his banker told him that dissolving Arctic Feather & Down — and losing all the jobs the company provided to the local economy — wouldn't be "civic-minded." The banker told Ed not to worry about overextending himself financially; Ed could count on a one-million-dollar line of credit from the bank, more if necessary. Reluctantly, Ed said he would be "civic-minded" — for one year. During that period of time, he would incorporate Arctic Feather & Down and offer shares to other Seattleites "who could better afford to carry this thing on than I could."

Backed by the million-dollar line of credit, Ed purchased materials and went into production of premium goose-down-insulated garments and heavy-duty sleeping bags. But soon after all these commitments were made, his banker told Ed that his credit line had been cut in half. Ed learned that the banker had other customers who were in financial trouble; the conservative bank directors reduced loan amounts with

all of the banker's accounts, including Eddie Bauer.

This blow was almost more than Ed could take. His physician told him that any more "unnecessary business burdens" could seriously affect his heart. With Sara Jane Smith's approval, Ed appointed a trustee, Dana Morrison, to liquidate both Arctic Feather & Down Co. and the store for the benefit of the bank and the creditors. Ed was virtually wiped out; his lone remaining asset was a modest farm at Bear Creek, east of Seattle. "I could see my life savings go down the drain. It was all so unnecessary and due entirely of the whim of a banker who, under the circumstances, was not being 'civic-minded.'"

He entered into licensing agreements with the trustee to protect the Eddie Bauer name by making sure that what Ed called "the Eddie Bauer package" — all patents, trademarks, trade names, copyrights, formulas, mailing lists — remained Ed's personal property and not included in the trust agreement. Arctic Feather & Down was eventually liquidated and the corporation dissolved, but the corporate name was transferred to Ed's nephew, Percy L. Yackel, who had been a manager of the company. The assets of Feathers, Inc., were sold. A license was given to Eddie Bauer, Inc., to operate Eddie Bauer Expedition Outfitters and Eddie Bauer Mail Order. For the use of the license, Ed was paid about $500 a month.

Faced with these pressures and setbacks, Ed sank deeper and deeper into depression. Extended rest was his doctor's prescription. By all reports, Stine was the tower of strength in the Bauer family at that time. "My mother was a real workhorse, and very strong," said Eddie C. Bauer, Ed and Stine's only child. "She grew vegetables and did all the butchering of the farm animals. She used to get up in the morning and milk the cow and then come in and fix breakfast." Stine, Ed wrote in his memoirs, "was an earthy person if there ever was one, blessed with exceptionally fine health and possessed with energy and vitality that I have never seen in any human being before or since. She was never one to be concerned about riches and the ordeal we were going through did not seem to bother her particularly. I am sure she would have been just as content living in a comfortable log cabin as in the finest of mansions."

With his business and health both ailing, Eddie Bauer needed help — not an easy admission for a proud man who had struggled, fought and worked for everything he had. Help did come, and from an unexpected source.

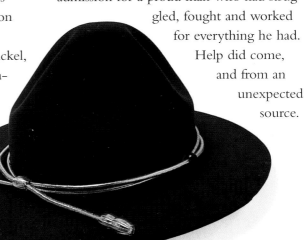

The 1966–67 American Antarctic Mountaineering Expedition used equipment supplied by Eddie Bauer Expedition Outfitters. The group was the first to conquer the 16,850-foot Vinson Massif, the highest summit in Antarctica. Down-filled products have always been strong sellers for the company. Ed particularly liked the imagery of this "sky-writing" treatment used in the 1960 catalog, right, and in many other promotional pieces.

CHAPTER THREE

BILL NIEMI AND THE POSTWAR YEARS

William F. Niemi, Sr., was born Franz Wilhold Niemiaho on July 14, 1904, in Everett, Washington, the fifth child (and the first born in the United States) of Frank and Hannah Niemiaho, whose last name was Americanized by an immigration officer at Ellis Island when they arrived from their native Finland at the turn of the century. The Niemis lived for several years on Whidbey Island in Puget Sound, where Frank was a tailor, before moving to Everett, a bustling timber and mill town about 30 miles north of Seattle.

In 1920, Bill quit school at the age of 16 and lied about his age to get into the navy. A seaman's life was rough and tumble in those days, when it was common practice for judges to offer young petty criminals the option of a tour of duty in the navy instead of a prison term. Bill survived because he could handle himself with his fists — he was champion of the Pacific Fleet in his 140-pound weight class — although by the time he left the navy four years later, at the age of 20, he had lost all of the bone and cartilage from the middle of his nose, which had been broken many times.

Following his tour of duty, Bill learned the electrical trade at the naval shipyard in Bremerton, west of Seattle on Puget Sound, where he lived from 1939 to 1942. During that time, he met and courted Louise Fitzwater, a legal secretary. "It was very common for them to have a date where my mother would bring a dinner and sit there while my father was wiring a house for extra pay," said his son, William F. Niemi, Jr. After they were married, Bill worked as a shipyard electrician.

In 1942, Bill's brother-in-law, Frank Lamphere, offered Bill a chance to buy Frank's Seattle cabaret, which had the tantalizing name of the Garden of Allah. Louise, a religious woman, strongly objected to her

Ed was always on the lookout for a new sport to promote; water-skiing was a typical example. In the early 1940s, a group of Seattleites invented the sport and quickly made it fashionable. Soon Ed was carrying water skis at Lohrer's, the sporting goods store that he helped finance in Seattle's University District. Imagine how much safer today's skis are than the ones pictured here which used sneakers and other lace-up footwear affixed to the wood skis.

husband's getting involved in a nightclub, much less one located on First Avenue, the city's bawdy boulevard of taverns, honky-tonks, strip joints, tattoo parlors and pawn shops, which drew battalions of servicemen seeking a variety of options for rest and relaxation. Despite his wife's protestations, the opportunity to have a business of his own was too important for Bill. He bought the Garden of Allah and maintained it as a thriving, if notorious, business. "Bill was a hard worker and he was smart," said Louise. "He had self-confidence you wouldn't believe. Never any fear at all."

"Bill was a helluva good guy," recalled Ted Van Theil, a hunting and fishing buddy who worked at Eddie Bauer's Sport Shop from 1931 to 1938. "He was a hard-working, hard-nosed, bull-headed guy."

An avid deer hunter and fisherman, Bill was a longtime customer of Eddie Bauer's Sport Shop, just a few blocks away from the Garden of Allah. Bill and Ed became hunting and fishing companions, despite the fact that "each one felt that his knowledge was superior to the other's," Louise recalled with a laugh. Eventually, the Bauer family and the Niemi family (including

daughter Sallie and Bill, Jr.) became close friends; the Niemis were frequent visitors to the Bauers' Bear Creek farm, where they pitched a tent among a grove of trees. Eddie C. Bauer and Bill, Jr., who were about the same age, "were always fishing in the creek that went through the farm," recalled Louise, who became a lifelong friend of Stine Bauer.

Louise continued her efforts to persuade her husband to find another line of work. In November 1947, when a buyer emerged for the Garden of Allah, Stine became Louise's most important ally in convincing

Bill to sell. "Stine was really the one who influenced Bill the most," recalled Louise. One evening, when the two couples were out to dinner, Stine privately told Bill that a cabaret was no atmosphere in which to raise children and suggested that Ed needed help with the business. Bill knew that Ed was in financial trouble, but wasn't sure he was the one to save his friend. He was the first to admit he knew nothing about merchandising and had never sold anything more complicated than a glass of beer. Stine pleaded with Bill, "You get up here and help Ed. He needs help.'"

Ed certainly did need help. His doctor insisted that he should concentrate on regaining his health and not deal with business matters. Arctic Feather & Down Co. was in receivership and was soon liquidated (along with Feathers, Inc.,) to pay off bankers and creditors; the retail store was close to bankruptcy, and Ed was in such dire financial straits that the Niemis stepped in to pay the Bauers' income and property taxes so they wouldn't lose their home. Ed was forced to sell most of his real estate properties (although he retained the option of buying them back within three years).

After Bill agreed to take over the business, he and Ed signed what would turn out to be a series of agreements. Under a license agreement drawn March 8, 1948, Ed gave Niemi permission to utilize certain of Ed's patents, trademarks and copyrighted material. In 1949, Ed transferred all of the common stock of Eddie Bauer, Inc., to Bill for one dollar and, in Ed's words "other valuable considerations," namely Ed's patents,

trade names, formulas, patterns, records, equipment, mailing lists, artwork and the commercial use of the Eddie Bauer name.

TURNING AROUND THE BUSINESS

Bill's first order of business was to deal with the $80,000 note that Eddie Bauer, Inc., owed Peoples National Bank. He convinced the bank to give him a year to pay it off. As he was the first to admit, Niemi didn't know much about retailing or merchandising, but he knew how to raise cash. To clear out the inventory in the retail store at Sixth and Union, he put every item in stock on display tables (which he built himself) and sold them for whatever cash he could raise. Although virtually everything sold, the presentation wasn't pretty, and the fastidious Eddie Bauer "just about died when he saw a bunch of bargain tables sitting out in the middle of his store," Louise recalled. "Bill told him, 'If you don't like the looks of it, then go on home.' Bill was a very strong person. If he wanted to go in a certain direction, it didn't matter who was standing in front of him." A year later, the bank note was paid off, and on June 1, 1950, a new entity was born — the William F. Niemi Co., doing business as Eddie Bauer Alaska Outfitters, a manufacturing and mail order business. According to a financial report from Dun & Bradstreet, the William F. Niemi Co. started the business with capital of $15,000.

On August 29, 1951, the Eddie Bauer company officially abandoned the retail store business when the inventory and

accounts receivable of the store were sold for $101,000 to Frederick & Nelson, which was then the premier department store in Seattle. While it did not buy the Eddie Bauer name as part of the deal, Frederick & Nelson, a division of Marshall Field & Co., was allowed to use "Eddie Bauer" in promoting the department for two years. Henry Allen, who arranged the deal with Niemi and managed the sporting goods department for Frederick & Nelson, remembers thinking they could have bought all the rights to the Eddie Bauer name for another $10,000. "We didn't buy the Bauer name because it wasn't worth anything in those days. The Frederick & Nelson name was a lot bigger."

In the early 1950s, Ed's vigor returned. "I could see hope for the future," he recalled. "I had been able to repurchase my farm and to make regular monthly payments on the sizable amount of business debts I had been responsible for through my personal guarantees to my suppliers. My desire was to prove the worth — the true worth — of the business I had been relieved of and the products I had created. I personally was determined to come back even stronger than before." To show people that he was back on his feet, Ed sold his secondhand pick-up truck and bought a shiny new Cadillac.

In April 1953, Bill Niemi performed what can only be described as a remarkable act of generosity: he dissolved the original William F. Niemi Co. and formed a new William F. Niemi Co. with Eddie Bauer as a fifty-fifty partner. Each man invested

Eddie Bauer's 1953 catalog, right, continued the oblong format of the company's first catalog, middle, which was issued in 1945. Early catalogs offered a handful of down-filled items, clothing, sleeping robes and sleeping bags, as well as apparel from other manufacturers. The down-insulated Kara Koram® parka, far right, was designed for a 1953 attempt to scale 28,250-foot Mount Godwin Austen (K-2) and became a bestseller.

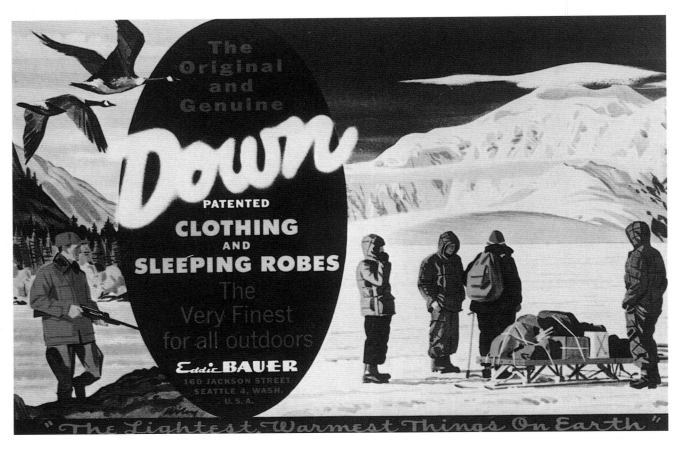

$44,000 for his share. In the new company, Niemi handled the financial side; Ed the manufacturing, merchandising and advertising. Their sewing/manufacturing operation (which Ed had set up prior to joining forces with Niemi) was headquartered in a rented 14,400-square-foot loft on the third floor of a building at 160 South Jackson Street, near the King Street railroad station, where they employed about 15 seamstresses. Ed made the garment patterns and, with the help of an assistant, built all of the sewing and cutting tables, conveyor boxes and

down-filling equipment.

The genesis of the first Eddie Bauer mailing list came from several shoe boxes stuffed with the names of some 14,000 loyal wartime mail order customers, many of them military officers and aviators who knew the Eddie Bauer name through the label in their flight suits and sleeping bags. Ed's insistence on using his labels had turned out to be a brilliant marketing coup.

By today's standards, early catalogs were modest. The first, issued in 1945, concentrated on Blizzard-Proof® products. By

1953, Eddie Bauer was producing a 28-page, 5 1/2 by 8 1/2-inch catalog containing down-insulated items, such as the Yukon® jacket (men's and women's styles), Skyliner® jacket, down vests, coats, pants and sleeping bags, as well as apparel from other manufacturers, such as Filson coats and Pendleton shirts. Business was profitable from the start, growing to about $50,000 in gross sales by 1953; by 1956, annual sales jumped tenfold to $500,000.

The company soon expanded to the fourth floor of the South Jackson Street

building, which became a minor tourist attraction for mail order customers coming through town on their way to Alaska and other rugged locales. So many people visited the shop that the company finally put aside a room where customers could try on jackets.

Two of the key employees during that time were Jack Abercrombie and Bob Lamphere. Abercrombie, who joined the Bauer retail store in 1946 after eight years in the navy, was the shipping clerk for mail order sales, as well as jack-of-all trades — handling the correspondence and helping

out wherever needed, from blowing down into garments to running a sewing machine. Lamphere, Niemi's nephew, was the production manager, overseeing the layout of fabrics and the down-filling process. From 1951 to 1953, Lamphere was a partner of Niemis in the business until his share was acquired by Eddie Bauer. "Bob and Jack were excellent managers, who gave their all," Ed wrote in his memoirs. "Their hours were unlimited and they watched over our business as though it was their own. To them belongs a great deal

of credit for the success of Eddie Bauer during the years 1950 to 1968."

Customers trusted the merchandise they bought from Eddie Bauer because they knew it had been thoroughly tested before it was ever offered in the catalog. Ed, Bill, Abercrombie and Lamphere lived the outdoors lifestyle and lived in the Eddie Bauer product. "What Ed and my father did, as a reflection of their personality, was to develop a quality product line that they would trust with the safety of their own family. That's what the company was built on," said

Bill Niemi, Jr. The company could back up its claims that a jacket or sleeping bag could keep the user warm and comfortable in extremely cold temperatures. Some tests were made in the field, others were done at the Diamond Ice & Cold Storage building in Seattle. "They would give us a locker big enough for us to spend the night in sleeping bags at 40 degrees below zero," recalled Abercrombie.

On a polar bear hunt in Alaska in March 1958, the elder Niemi saw firsthand dramatic proof of the quality of Eddie Bauer garments. A plane piloted by Jack Hovland, a member of Niemi's hunting party, skidded on to an ice pack and then sank in Arctic water, 60 miles off Point Barrow. Hovland was lost in the water, but the passenger, Tony Sulak, a Seattle tool-and-die-operator, smashed the ice with his fists to clear a channel, and swam 250 feet against a violent wind to a point of land where Niemi and Frank Gregory, an Alaskan pilot, could rescue him. Sulak credited his rescue to the bravery of Niemi and Gregory, his will to live, his physical endurance and the buoyancy of his Eddie Bauer down underwear, which helped keep him afloat during the 20 minutes he was exposed to the 18-degrees-below-zero temperatures.

EXPEDITION OUTFITTERS

In the early 1950s, Himalayan expeditions became popular among serious American mountain climbers, who turned to Eddie Bauer Alaska Outfitters for their garments, sleeping bags and tents. The first such

Customers trusted the merchandise they bought from Eddie Bauer because they knew it had been thoroughly tested before it was offered for sale. Some tests were made in the field, others were done in cold-storage lockers. Bauer employees Jack Abercrombie and Bob Lamphere would spend a night in sleeping bags at temperatures as low as 40 degrees below zero testing the bags.

Eddie Bauer has supplied clothing and gear for mountaineering expeditions arranged by worthy organizations and has served as corporate sponsor. One of those treks was "Project Pelion," which symbolized equal opportunity and access for all. In celebration of the International Year of Disabled Persons in 1981, a team of climbers who were physically challenged ascended 14,410-foot Mt. Rainier. Some climbers had artificial limbs, others were deaf, blind or otherwise disabled; all had the determination to get to the top. Of the 11 climbers nine made it all the way.

Serious American mountain climbers depended on Eddie Bauer for their gear. In 1963, Jim Whittaker of Seattle, right, became the first American to reach the top of Everest, the tallest mountain in the world. Chris Kopczynski of Spokane, above, became in 1981 the ninth American to reach the summit of Everest while climbing with the American Medical Expedition.

expedition was a 1953 attempt to scale 28,250-foot Mount Godwin Austen (K-2), which was then the world's highest unconquered peak. The nine-man team included three veteran Seattle climbers: Pete Schoening, Dee Molenaar and Bob Craig. Ome Daiber, the Seattle mountaineer who had helped Ed produce the original Skyliner® jacket, introduced Schoening to Ed, Bill Niemi, Bob Lamphere and Jack Abercrombie, who produced for the expedition a down-insulated parka, which revived the Kara Koram® name, and became a bestseller.

From then on, "whenever climbers were planning an expedition, they would tell Ed the month they planned to be there and what the weather conditions were going to be, and leave it up to Ed to design the garment or sleeping bag with the right amount of insulation," said John Kime, the longtime copywriter for the Eddie Bauer catalog, who began with the company in 1960 and remains as senior advertising consultant.

After the K-2 climb, the company provided gear for expeditions to such famous peaks as Gasherbrum (Hidden Peak) and Dhaulagiri, under conditions that pushed the adventurers and their equipment to the limit. For example, during a 1955 Himalayan climb, one man suffered a heart attack and spent the night at 24,600 feet, lying on the ice without a sleeping bag. His

survival was credited to the protection provided by his Eddie Bauer down-quilted jacket and pants.

Without doubt, the most notable expedition outfitted by Eddie Bauer was the successful 1963 Mt. Everest expedition, when Jim Whittaker of Seattle became the first American to reach the top of the tallest mountain in the world.

Acclaim from experts for the quality of Eddie Bauer equipment became common, and its performance created "word of mouth" advertising that spread the Eddie Bauer reputation beyond North America. "The Sherpas have become connoisseurs of mountaineering equipment," a member of the 1964 Oregon Himalayan Expedition observed. "Our stature as an expedition rose in their eyes when they saw we had Bauer equipment." When Nicholas Clinch led the 1966-67 American Antarctic Mountaineering Expedition that conquered the four tallest peaks on the frozen continent, he wrote from near the South Pole, "It would be impossible to survive without our superb Bauer down equipment...the

finest we have ever seen.... My Bauer down jacket is my happiness and security blanket."

Such notoriety firmly established the "expedition-tested" stature of Eddie Bauer products and greatly enhanced the company's reputation as "America's premier outdoor outfitter." Subsequent expeditions invariably found ways to improve the products, which would then appear in the next series of Eddie Bauer catalogs.

Beginning in the mid-1950s, Eddie Bauer emerged as a major outfitter for ranchers, veterinarians, utility linemen, railyard workers, highway patrolmen, mineral geologists and many others whose occupations exposed them to cold weather.

The company's first large-scale industrial outfitting task was providing goose-down outerwear for the pilots, air crew members and maintenance personnel of Alaska-based Wien Airlines. Eddie Bauer products were also specially designed for the construction workers and operators of America's Arctic defense installations — the Distant Early Warning (DEW) Military Defense Link — to protect them from frigid weather in an icy wilderness that few but Eskimos had penetrated before. For the 1957-58 U.S. Geophysical Year expeditions to both the Arctic and Antarctica, Bauer outfitted 20 scientists (the first men to winter at the

South Pole) who spent six months working in temperatures that averaged 70 degrees below zero and dropped to 110 degrees below zero. Two decades later, the 70,000 workers who built the 800-mile Trans-Alaska Pipeline were outfitted in customized parkas and other gear. Alyeska Pipeline Service Company's oilfield crews and Prudhoe Bay workers also wore Eddie Bauer outerwear.

ENTER THE SONS

In the late 1950s, two new partners were added — Eddie C. Bauer and William F. Niemi, Jr.

Eddie C., who graduated from the University of Washington in 1959 and then enlisted in the army, was given an 18 percent ownership out of his father's half of the company.

Bill, Jr., earned a B.A. from Harvard University and an M.A. in electronic data processing from the Sloan School of Industrial Management at the Massachusetts Institute of Technology and was anxious to join the company. (Bill, Sr., gave his son 5 of his 50 percent share.) Even as a small child, young Niemi would tell people he "was going to be a feather merchant just like his father," his mother recalled. "That was his goal. He just loved it and he was good at it." Like his father, Bill, Jr., was an avid outdoorsman. He was captain of Harvard's ski team, shot grouse in Scotland, fished for marlin off Panama and skippered his own boat in the 4,000-mile Cape Town-to-Rio race from Africa

to South America.

In 1961, the South Jackson Street building was sold, with manufacturing and mail order operations moving to an old wooden building at 417 East Pine Street and Summit Avenue. To make absolutely sure all visitors recognized that this was a serious expedition outfitter, a full mount of a Kodiak bear taken by the elder Niemi in earlier years stood guard in the small foyer.

The Pine Street space included a modest factory outlet store where "It was nothing to see customers lying around on the floor, being measured to make sure that they fit inside sleeping bags," recalled Deanna Lieske Norsen, who was a secretary in the advertising department. "When the store got busy during the Christmas shopping season, Mr. Bauer rounded us all up and took us out on the sales floor to help customers." There was no cash register and all of the orders were written up by hand. "People were absolutely amazed when Mr. Bauer would write up the order and sign it 'E. Bauer.' They couldn't believe that *the* Eddie Bauer had been helping them. He was such a genuine man with customers. He was very interested in what they were going to be using the equipment for and where they were going."

Eddie C. Bauer recalled that, "My dad was almost fanatical about customer service, and he personally answered every customer letter of complaint. He regarded any person who was dissatisfied as a real opportunity to make a friend. I remember one time in the 1960s, a man brought in a tattered old sleeping bag that he had bought from dad

in the thirties. He said he wasn't very happy with it because the zipper wasn't working right. The people in the store thought the guy was not being fair. They got dad, and he just said, 'Well, would you like a new one or do you want your money back?' The guy said, 'I'll take a new one.' So, they gave him a brand new one."

With the move to Pine Street, Bill McGuire was brought in as director of research and development for clothing, footwear and fishing. "Bill was one of the most creative people I ever met in my life," recalled Cam Sigler, who filled many production, sales and management positions during his career at Eddie Bauer, the last as product manager for hardware. "He designed a special line of knives that was being specially made for Eddie Bauer by Gerber Manufacturing. Instead of just putting the design on paper, Bill carved models of the knives out of balsa wood. They were sharp enough to cut you." McGuire called Eddie Bauer apparel "the best stuff you could get. We used only the best manufacturers. When they put a button on a garment, it stayed there. When we put something in the catalog, we could back it almost for life because it was that good; you couldn't wear it out. You were proud of the Eddie Bauer label." By the early 1960s, the catalog had expanded to 80 pages, covering a product line that included a wide variety of down-insulated coats, shirts, vests, underwear, mittens, caps, sleeping bags, pillows and comforters, as well as footwear and socks; tents, air mattresses and packboards; and tools such as saws, axes,

One of many loyal Eddie Bauer customers was Father Bernard Hubbard, the famed "Glacier Priest," who piloted his plane across northern Alaska with his Eddie Bauer down-insulated coats, vests and sleeping bags. Father Hubbard's letters of praise for Eddie Bauer products were printed in company catalogs.

March 2, 1962

Dear Eddie, Your letter came today and will be answered soon. Meanwhile I think this photograph with your Eddie Bauer coat should satisfy the picture you wish for the catalog. You have my full permission to use it. B.R. Hubbard S.J.

QUALITY SPEAKS FOR ITSELF

he most gratifying evidence of a job well done comes from appreciative letters from satisfied customers. Over the years, Eddie Bauer has received testimonials from people like Charles Lindbergh, who made the first nonstop solo flight from New York to Paris, and Jim Whittaker, the first American to reach the top of Mt. Everest.

Whittaker, who was equipment coordinator for the 1963 expedition, which was outfitted by Eddie Bauer, wrote, "Without exception, every article of down equipment we used carried the Bauer label... and it was superb."

In 1979, a World War II veteran extolled the virtues of the Skyliner® jacket that he wore on 13 combat missions in the Pacific. He wrote, "We had little heat in our plane at 25,000 to 35,000 feet and the jacket kept me warm." He donated his Skyliner® to the Bauer archives.

That tradition of dependability continues today. In 1994, a customer authored an appreciative letter about how an Eddie Bauer Legend 1AAA penlight helped get his family through the first few hours after the January 17 Los Angeles earthquake, which occurred at 4:30 a.m. As he and his family huddled together in the darkness, without power, their only source of illumination was the penlight. With the tiny flashlight, "I read to my children to calm their nerves, and later used it to gather our other emergency equipment. That frightening morning, this bright and rugged little light turned

Scotts Cove
Darien, Conn.
Nov. 20, 1960

Dear Mary:

Here is the Bauer catalogue I spoke about. Unfortunately this one does not carry the down quilts; but you could get information about them by writing to the Bauer people. The Bauer down products are excellent -- used extensively in the far north. The quilts would be light-weight, and much warmer than wool -- but I don't know what kind of covering they would have from an appearance standpoint. I suggest being careful about that unless you are willing to end up with khaki!

It was grand to have dinner with you and Dana the other night at Englewood. And my uncle and I enjoyed the apples, pears, and pie very much -- he asks me to send his thanks along with mine.

Best to you always,

Charles

I finally got a letter from my wife! One to four -- that's really quite a record for a husband.

A beaming Charles Lindbergh stands with his new bride, Anne Morrow Lindbergh, a few years after his historic 1927 flight that captured the imagination of the world. Anne often accompanied her husband on flights, recording data and keeping journal notes. While the background of the 1960 letter, left, is unknown, it's clear that Lindbergh was a satisfied customer.

NO CHICKEN FEATHERS

O ne afternoon, Mr. Bauer came charging through the office," former secretary Deanna Lieske Norsen recalled. "He was upset because there was an old truck parked out in front of the store that had big wooden crates for holding chickens. There weren't any chickens in the crates, but wind was blowing chicken feathers all around the front of the store. Mr. Bauer was just having a fit. He said, 'Somebody get that truck off the street.' He was afraid that everybody would think we were putting chicken feathers in comforters and sleeping bags. We had so many laughs about that."

compasses and knives. The company produced 60 percent of all the hunting, camping and general outdoor recreational clothing and equipment it sold. (Goose-down products made up the largest company-manufactured category.) Most of the other items sold under the Bauer label were designed and produced exclusively for Bauer by outside firms.

The catalog was Ed's baby, and gave him a forum to expound upon the superior qualities of goose-down insulation. John Kime recalled, "Ed was absolutely in love with his 'Eddie Bauerisms' about down: 'It prevents clothing fatigue' and 'it's light but tough.'" Although he had a limited education, Ed possessed a punster's feel for the language, authoring lines like "bootsies for frigid tootsies," "take a tip from the birds, go light," and "what's up with down."

Sprinkled throughout the catalog were letters of testimonial from satisfied customers, such as Father Hubbard, the Glacier Priest. Typical was this letter from Warren Page, the shooting editor of *Field & Stream* magazine: "I have been kept warm by Bauer jackets over much of the world — from Alaska and all the mountain country of our own Northwest, even to Africa, where it can get mighty frosty around dawn."

In the early 1960s, the company expanded from one annual catalog to three — spring, fall and Christmas — as new items were added. Each new item was voted on by a committee comprised of the Bauers, the Niemis, McGuire and John Kime, who would convene in Ed's office for a decision-

making process that the participants remember as excruciating. "Let's say someone presented a tweed hat," Bill Niemi, Jr., recalled. "They would make a case for why we ought to have it in the catalog. Then we would all discuss it and vote on it. Ed kept track of the vote on a yellow pad. After he announced the results, we would decide what the sales forecast would be for the first year, so that we knew what to order. He would go around the room and ask everybody for their estimate of the number we would sell. Then, he would add each estimate up and average it. That was the sales forecast. My father got so disgusted that one day, when Ed asked him how many we were going to sell on an item, dad just said, 'Bingo.' After that, this was known as 'The Bingo Game.'"

OVERWHELMED BY GROWTH

By the mid-1960s, the company was pulling in more than $2 million a year, and it was growing. The mailing list expanded to 100,000. The factory, which employed 60 persons year round, bought almost one-third of the Western world's supply of goose down. But the demands on the business were beginning to be overwhelming. Bill McGuire recalled that he couldn't get Ed to hire enough people. "We'd put all the orders in a big barrel. I'd wait until Ed walked by and then I'd have a man stir the orders in the barrel. Ed would say, 'McGuire, what is he doing?' I said, 'Ed, we got 500 orders yesterday, and we can only do 50 because of the amount of

CELEBRITY CUSTOMERS

*E*ddie Bauer's reputation for authenticity attracted a wide variety of noted people from all over the world: Eleanor Roosevelt (who bought Indian-knit sweaters for gifts), Clark Gable, Will Rogers, Fatty Arbuckle, Lou Gehrig, Admiral Richard Byrd, General James Doolittle, the Marx Brothers, John Wayne, Roy Rogers and several duPonts and Boeings, among others. For many years, he kept a handwritten note from the author Zane Gray, (who in the 1920s used to buy supplies at Ed's store on Seneca Street) apologizing for a late payment.

Jack Abercrombie recalled the night he was about to close the store on Sixth and Union when he received a telephone call from an official at The Boeing Company. "They said they had a distinguished person in town who wanted to drop down and make a purchase and asked if would we be willing to wait for him. The fellow purchased a sleeping bag and a garment, totaling about $200, which was a lot of money in those days. He wrote out a check and I had to take a second look because the signature said 'Charles Lindbergh.'"

In the 1960s, the king and queen of Nepal came to the store on their way back from big-game hunting in Alaska. "They had been Bauer customers for many years and wanted a tour of the place," recounted Bill Niemi, Jr. "Here come the limousines, the police escort and a half a dozen secret service agents. After the tour, to commemorate the visit, we gave them

S'TINE AND MRS. "LOU GEHRIG"

camelhair overcoats with down liners."

The king wanted to meet Eddie Bauer himself. "Mr. Bauer was as fascinated as the rest of us, but he was shy and modest," recalled Deanna Norsen. "He said, 'I didn't wear a suit; it's not necessary.' Finally, the people from the company convinced him that he really should go out and meet the king. He wasn't into that sort of thing. He didn't find himself famous at all."

On a fishing trip, Stine maneuvers a net for her friend Eleanor Gehrig, wife of Hall of Fame baseball star Lou Gehrig. This picture is from Eddie's hand-written scrapbook in which he kept important photos.

people we've got. So, the man stirs the orders and we serve the ones that come to the top.'"

The company sometimes found itself overrun by its pre-computer-era order-processing system. When an order arrived by mail, a couple of secretaries typed out the customer's request on a company form, which was paper-clipped together with the customer's letter and check and sent in a box to the warehouse, where the workers filled the order. Often a customer would have to settle for his second or third choice in color.

"Nobody had any idea of what the real demand for anything was," noted the younger Niemi. "I remember one Christmas in 1963 or 1964, we had to send back to the customers half a million dollars in uncashed checks. We told them, 'Sorry, we're out. Could you order later in the year?'"

Cash flow was erratic because most of Eddie Bauer's sales were made during fall and winter. "We didn't have much to sell people for the summer and spring," recalled John Kime. "In January, we had to get a bundle of money together to buy fabric, zippers and everything else, manufacture the stuff and put it in storage for the big sale season, which started in September. You had this stuff sitting there, dead, dull, producing no revenue, for probably seven months a year."

The name and address of each customer receiving a catalog had to be typed out on a 3" x 2" steel Addressograph plate. When the catalogs came back from the printer, the addresses were added with the

Addressograph plate — a long, tedious process. In these pre-zip code days, the post office required addressed catalogs to be sorted out by state and then by major cities within the state. If there were at least five catalogs going to each city, they had to be alphabetized, grouped together and labeled with the name of the city. Before being mailed, each of these catalog groupings was wrapped up in a bundle with string. "It became a real family affair; we had everybody doing it," Bill Niemi, Jr., recalled.

"We would start out on Friday and would work around the clock until Sunday when our fingers were bleeding from tying the strings."

Clearly, if the Eddie Bauer company was going to achieve its potential, it was going to have to move into the modern era of business. That meant being armed with up-to-date information and order-processing systems, sufficient working capital to expand and one clear direction. That also meant a changing of the guard.

Although Himalayan expeditions are the best known of the many mountaineering adventures outfitted by Eddie Bauer, the company also sponsored treks to South America, such as the American Andes Expedition and the Inca Highway Expedition.

Beginning in the early 1950s, Himalayan expeditions became popular. Many climbers relied on Eddie Bauer garments, sleeping bags and tents. All-important word-of-mouth advertising spread the Bauer reputation beyond North America. In 1980, Eddie Bauer outfitted members of the American Women's Expedition to Dhaulagiri (above), the 26,810-foot peak in Nepal.

From the day Eddie Bauer wrote Our Creed and Our Guarantee, the company has had a single-minded dedication to providing reliable, durable products. The continuous testing of materials used in Eddie Bauer garments assures that they meet exacting performance standards. The labels used by the company, right, still contain a version of Ed's signature, which has been used in many company logos over the years, including the stamp below.

CHAPTER FOUR

ENTERING THE MODERN ERA

Throughout the first decade of their partnership, Eddie Bauer and William F. Niemi, Sr., "each prospered handsomely, accumulated a sizable net worth and had excellent banking connections with ample credit for any of our needs," Ed wrote in his memoirs. The partners were content to take their share of the profits (which had become substantial) and enjoy hunting and fishing, which were the other most important activities in their lives.

Although the Niemis and the Bauers lived a few doors away from each other in Bellevue, and Stine and Louise were close friends, the same couldn't be said for Ed

and Bill. Although they hunted and socialized together with their wives, "They weren't the kind of personalities that would become really best friends," said Bill, Jr. Nevertheless, for much of their partnership, they complemented each other well. Ed described Bill as "ultraconservative" and "a tight money man," who was "very careful of every dollar spent." Those traits made Niemi "an excellent person for me to work with, because I had a tendency to be a 'plunger.'" What Ed meant was that while he preferred to build up inventories and explore new lines, Niemi wanted to make sure the money was in the bank first.

Their differences grew wider over the years, and by 1968, when annual sales were approaching $5 million, the company, "had grown to a size where it was getting away from these two old warhorses," said Bill, Jr. The company required more professional management and financial planning. "Neither Ed nor my father had any kind of formal education to speak of. My father was getting to the point where he found it difficult to contribute to the business because he didn't understand the demands it was making. The same thing with Ed. You can only get so far on instinct and hard work. There were a lot of pressures and

In the late 1950s, William F. Niemi, Jr., became a partner in the company. In 1968, he and his father bought out the 50 percent interest of Eddie Bauer and his son, Eddie C., for $1.5 million. Niemi, Jr., led the company through its acquisition by General Mills, Inc., and left a few years later in 1975. Eddie posed for this promotional shot, right, in 1983, after he retired.

conflicts. It just didn't work. Toward the end, it was a real knock-down drag-out fight."

"I would never go into business with a friend after seeing the experience they had," said Eddie C. "Dad and Bill would get along fine if they were on a hunting trip. But when business became involved, there was a real dichotomy."

The younger Niemi, who was anxious to make his mark, saw that the company had barely scratched its potential. "We had a tremendous opportunity because we had a strong reputation, a wonderful heritage and products that had a powerful place in the

market," he recalled. "When you contribute to people's lives by providing enjoyment in the outdoors and keeping them warm, you build a relationship that is unique; it's far different from just selling them a shirt."

One avenue for capitalizing on that relationship was to expand into retail, a move that was supported by the senior Niemi but fiercely opposed by Ed, who preferred staying strictly with mail order. As far as Ed was concerned, once he had sold the remainder of the inventory from his last store in 1951 to Frederick & Nelson, he was out of the retail business for good — except for the limited retail sales from the company store.

He once told John Pfeffer, the company accountant, "We can't manufacture enough now for what we can sell, so why have retail stores?"

Eventually, Bill Niemi, Sr., had had enough. He told his son, "I've spent a lot of money on your education. You've done pretty well. I'm tired of fighting with Ed. He's all yours. I'm going fishing." Niemi didn't return to the company for about six weeks, and even after that, he was never again intimately involved in its operations.

Soon after, one day in the early part of 1968, Eddie C. called Bill Niemi, Jr., and told him that the Bauer family had decided

to sell their 50 percent interest in the company. Their asking price was $1.5 million — in cash. Niemi, Jr., after agreeing on the details, asked Eddie C. how long the offer would stand. The answer was 10 days. If the Niemis could not raise the cash within that time, the Bauer family would buy out the Niemi family.

Faced with such a tight deadline, the younger Niemi hustled to raise the cash. He was able to convince Peoples National Bank to put up $1 million and Smith, Barney & Co. the remaining $500,000 (in exchange for shares of common stock).

When the sale was finalized in June 1968, Eddie Bauer walked away from the company he had founded nearly a half-century before. "Selling out was hard for dad," recalled his son. "I think he wanted to continue. My preference, for personal reasons, was not to." After the sale, Ed "always kept busy," continued Eddie C. "He did a lot more fishing, hunting and bird shooting. He continued to raise Labrador retrievers, a breed that he introduced to the Pacific Northwest, and create new products. He invented a trolling lure, the B&B flasher, which he patented. He certainly maintained a strong personal interest in the company and continued to test products for them, but it wasn't for pay; it was more of an indirect role."

Regarding his retirement, Ed used to enjoy telling this story on himself: Soon after selling his share in the company, Ed took a fishing trip for king salmon on Cape Flattery, on Puget Sound. There, a three-year-old Macaw Indian girl came up to

EDDIE BAUER, DOG BREEDER

*E*d had loved dogs ever since he was a teenager, when he owned a hunting dog named Speed. In 1930, when he returned to Seattle from a hunting trip to Alberta, Canada, he brought with him an outstanding gun dog named Blackie, the very first Labrador retriever in Washington State. From that day on, he was a serious breeder, starting a bloodline he called Wanapum, named

after an eastern Washington Indian tribe. Blackie was mated to a bitch imported from England, which produced eight litters of top-flight gun dogs that Ed gave to hunting companions in Alberta, the Dakotas, Manitoba, Idaho and Oregon.

After he retired, Ed spent a lot of time at DeWitt's Redmond Kennels, in Redmond, Washington, where he would supervise the breeding and feed the

dogs. "He was a student of the game," recalled Eddie DeWitt, who with his wife, Kay, raised and trained many of the dogs in the Wanapum line for Ed. "He could look at a dog's pedigree and

WASHINGTON RETRIEVER CLUB
PICNIC TRIALS

FIRST PLACE
DERBY

prove to you why that pedigree was good because it had all the top females in the country," remembered Kay DeWitt. "He loved to talk on the telephone about dogs for hours and hours to people all over the country. His telephone bill must have been out of this world."

Deanna Lieske Norsen, Ed's former secretary, fondly recalled Ed's "wonderful old black Labrador retriever mother dog named Lady Dart," who would often accompany Ed to the office. "When she had puppies, he'd invite me out to his house in Bellevue, and we'd record their proper names and papers and send the

information to the American Kennel Club in New York."

In 1974, Ed was named "Retriever Breeder of the Year" by the Professional Retrievers Trainers Association — the first year the sterling silver trophy was awarded. The inscription cited "Dart of Netley Creek," whose offspring accumulated the most points in the 1974 Open and Amateur All Age Competition. Dart's mating with a dog named Super Chief, which was owned by Louise and August Belmont (owner of New York's Belmont Raceway), produced some of the top Labrador lines of all time.

In 1972, two other Wanapum-line pups, Wanapum Lucky Yo Yo and Cody of Wanapum, at three years of age, were the youngest retrievers qualified for that year's national championship. In 1973, Wanapum Lucky Yo Yo sold for $22,000, which was at the time the highest price ever paid for a dog — a distinction that earned it a place in the Guinness Book of Records. Cannonball Kate, a descendant of Wanapum Sheba, who was a descendant of Dart, still holds the record for the highest one-season total of accumulated points, open and amateur, for any Labrador female in the United States.

Ed was named "Retriever Breeder of the Year" by the Professional Retrievers Trainers Association. At right is Ed's dog Blackie, the first Labrador retriever brought into the state of Washington.

THE LEGEND OF EDDIE BAUER

him, kissed his cheek and said "Grandpas know everything, don't they?"

Ed laughed and replied, "They sure do. Who told you?"

"Mamma did," she said.

"Some grandpas don't know when to quit working," an amused Ed told her.

"Do you?" she asked.

"Yeah," Ed said with a chuckle, "I just did!"

A NEW COMPANY

The dawn of the company as we know it today began officially on May 29, 1968, (a few days before the sale was finalized) when it was incorporated as Eddie Bauer, Inc., succeeding the William F. Niemi, Inc., partnership, which did business under the name Eddie Bauer Expedition Outfitters. Thirty-year-old Bill Niemi, Jr., became company president; his father, chairman. Ronald C. Buehner, an M.I.T. classmate of Niemi, Jr., was executive vice president.

"Bill, Jr., set the course and got us to thinking about what potential there really was out there," said Ken Wherry, who is currently a senior vice president. Ken is an important source of knowledge because he has been with the company for the past 25 years.

With company operations scattered all around Seattle in five different buildings, the need to consolidate into one location was obvious. The new executive team coveted a building on Airport Way in South Seattle. The two-story structure was owned by Western Electric, Inc., which was asking for

$3.5 million — a price that was considerably more than the company could afford because of the expenses incurred in the cash buyout to Ed and Eddie C. Bauer.

Undaunted, Niemi and Henry Broderick, a Seattle real estate executive, flew to Western Electric's New York City headquarters for an appointment with that firm's head of real estate. "We made a proposal for about $1.6 million," Niemi recalled. "There was an additional piece of land that we were going to spin off, so we figured that we would be in for about $1.2 million. We made the presentation and [the Western Electric executive] didn't give us the time of day. But he felt sorry for us, having traveled all the way from Seattle, so he invited us to have lunch with him in the executive dining room before we got back on the plane. While we were sitting at a table, a very distinguished gray-haired gentleman came over with his tray and asked if he could join us. He turned out to be the legal counsel for Western Electric. It also turned out he had been an Eddie Bauer customer for 20 years. So, he took over and swept us right up to his office. He went out of his way to give us an extremely favorable price and terms because he believed in the company. As the years passed, we had many similar experiences that brought home to us the power of the Eddie Bauer name."

The Airport Way facility, which was built on 4.5 acres, gave the company 25,000 square feet of office space for general administrative purposes and customer service; 35,000 square feet for manufacturing and 71,000 square feet for warehousing and

distributing inventory. (To meet increased demand, a 28,000-square-foot subsidiary plant was later opened at Wetumpka, Alabama.) The company leased a computer and, over time, developed software programs for mail order processing, zip-coding, sales forecasting, inventory analysis, tracking manufacturing costs and accounting. Despite the high-tech trappings, Eddie Bauer retained its folksy flavor. Deanna Lieske Norsen, who was a secretary for the company from 1967 through 1976, worked on the second floor, which also housed manufacturing operations. "At 3 o'clock, when those people finished work," she recalled, "the doors would open and the down feathers would fly."

When Eddie Bauer left the company, he took with him his expertise in marketing and catalog production. Niemi turned the responsibility for the spring 1969 catalog over to an advertising agency, and the results were "a disaster," he recalled. "We ended up solving that by hiring Ken Wherry," who was a specialist in graphics and catalog production.

"The catalog was the lifeblood of the Eddie Bauer business," said Wherry. "Farming it out was like cutting off the tap to the cash flow. I brought it back in-house because we had the people here to make it work. John Kime, specifically, was an incredibly key player."

Prior to joining Bauer, Wherry was general manager of Jafco, a Seattle-based general merchandise discount mail order and retail chain, which had a large showroom at Westlake Avenue and Mercer Street, kitty-corner to the Eddie Bauer offices on Republican Street. Under Wherry's direction, Jafco began to share time on Bauer's newly installed IBM computer for processing Jafco's quarter-million-customer mailing list. (That was not Wherry's first exposure to the Eddie Bauer operation. After graduating from the University of Washington in the early 1950s, he sold printing to Ed

hired to take Bauer back into the retail business. "Retail gives you an ability to test some products and to market other products that are easier to sell at retail than through mail order," said Niemi. "People are more prone to order goods through the mail if they know that they have the option of returning them to the retail store if they have some problems in size."

In March of 1970, in one of the most pivotal decisions in the history of the company, the new Eddie Bauer regime opened its first large store on Third Avenue and Virginia Street in downtown Seattle. In addition to the classic Eddie Bauer products, such as the Skyliner® jacket, the Cruiser® sleeping bag and assorted expedition-caliber tents, the store had fully stocked fishing and gun shops that carried premium brands for demanding sportsmen. "Without question, it was one of the best outdoor stores in the country," said Cam Sigler, the store's first manager. In its first year, the store recorded about $900,000 in sales volume despite a near-depression in the local economy brought about by massive layoffs at The Boeing Company, the region's largest employer.

Classes were conducted in flycasting and other outdoor activities by Bauer people,

when the company was located at 417 East Pine Street.)

Wherry decided to join Eddie Bauer because "I saw a company that was on the edge of stepping out and growing the business. The early days were incredibly exciting, but I knew that before I joined. In fact, that was one of the reasons that I joined."

Besides his catalog expertise, Wherry was

Company headquarters on Seattle's Airport Way, above, in the late 1960s. The new Eddie Bauer regime opened its first large store on Third Avenue and Virginia Street, right, in 1970.

who were not just order-takers, but actual users of the products they sold. "We had the most knowledgeable salespeople in the country," said Sigler. As an ad of that era said, "To work indoors at Eddie Bauer, you have to be an outdoors person," which meant being well versed in how the gear performed. Goods for backpacking, hiking and camping — from pocket-sized stoves to expedition-quality tents — were developed and thoroughly tested under real conditions by Eddie Bauer people. Groups of managers participated in company-sponsored climbs of Mt. Rainier, led by Lou Whittaker, the

legendary mountain guide. Every manager was required to take at least one trip a year to a hunting club at Moses Lake, in eastern Washington, where the company had a corporate membership.

"It didn't matter whether or not an employee ever put a shotgun in his hands. It was important for him to understand the product he was selling, which is why we had such a tremendously loyal customer following," said Bill Niemi, Jr., who described the company in those days as "not really a job, but almost a religion. Bauer was a desirable place to work. I remember one

young man who held an M.B.A., who wanted a job with us and didn't care what level he entered on. He was quite willing to sweep the floors to start. We turned him into a file clerk, and he eventually advanced up the ranks."

Vendors who wanted to get their products in an Eddie Bauer catalog were required to go through some exacting paces. "If a vendor walked in with a product, we didn't ask how we could buy it cheaper, we looked to see how we could make it better," said Sigler. "We used to drive companies crazy; we'd tear the stuff

A **Seattle-based syndicate sponsored** *Intrepid* **in the 1974 America's Cup trials, and her crew wore Eddie Bauer gear.** *Intrepid* **had won the coveted cup in 1967 and 1970, but a broken turnbuckle eliminated her from the 1974 selection races.**

Field testing has always been part of the Eddie Bauer tradition. The more severe the environment, the better Bauer quality assurance people like it. This climber, wearing a version of the "Field Tester" patch, tries out a new expedition outfit under real conditions.

This Fieldwear is for the Birds!

Goose Down Trail Shirt

JUST ARRIVED!
Big, Tough, Brawny Boots for Backpackers, Hikers, Climbers, Mountaineers.

For a Special Kind of Man!

Ad reprints, left, show various Bauer products. They directed readers to the catalog or to retail stores. Many Eddie Bauer catalogs, like the ones below, feature commissioned paintings which become part of the company's permanent art collection.

apart to make sure it was made properly." Each product was thoroughly tested and used — perhaps for as long as a year — before Bauer would offer it to its customers. "We never wanted a customer to be the field tester on a product," said Sigler. "I wanted it used in the environment the customer would use it in. We would send a tent or a cooking utensil to a guy who guided on the Rogue River and Deschutes all summer. He'd make more use of it in a month than most people would in a lifetime. If he tore it up, you'd go back to the drawing board."

Some products slipped through the cracks. Sigler recalled getting some letters of complaint from customers about a flotation coat that the company was selling. So, one day, he donned some old clothes, put the coat on, and jumped into the pond on the Redmond headquarters campus. "It didn't float," Sigler recalled. "It was an open-cell foam garment and it got so heavy, I could hardly pick my arms up. I had to be pulled out of the pond."

Sigler sank because the Europe-based manufacturer had changed the garment's initial specifications. The sample garment that the Bauer buyers had been first shown — the one on which they had based their buying decision — was constructed of closed-cell foam, which made the coat float indefinitely. When the buyers discovered that the manufacturers had substituted cheaper open-cell foam, which absorbed water like a sponge, Bauer dropped the product.

The aggressive young Bauer executives saw they had an opportunity to dramatically expand the company's market share of high-quality hunting, camping and general out-door recreational clothing and equipment. But the company's potential far exceeded its ability to finance it. Although earnings were strong — more than $500,000 in 1970 on sales of $9.1 million — they were not enough to pay off what the company owed to Peoples National Bank and Western Electric and also to finance increased prod-uct output — not to mention the costs of building, leasing and buying inventory for the new retail stores it wanted to open in major markets around the country.

With this need to raise capital, the decision was made to take the company public in the spring of 1970 with the sale of 250,000 shares of stock. But just as they were about to make the offering public, the stock market went south. Smith, Barney & Co., the under-writer, recommended post-poning the offering and trying again at a later date so that the stock could maintain its price.

"I was faced with a dilem-ma," Niemi recalled. "I didn't have an alternate plan. I was going to have to slow down this juggernaut and we would have to live within our means — our operating income. We had a

sophisticated, marketable product and a group in high gear. I thought that slowing things down would affect the spirit of the company because rapid growth meant greater opportunity for everybody. We had to keep them there. We couldn't mark time, waiting for the stock market to make up its mind."

General Mills, Inc., had first expressed interest in buying the company as far back as 1966 — a time when the trend among food conglomerates was to diversify into non-food product categories. During this era, the Minneapolis-based company also acquired Izod sportswear, Talbots (the women's wear retail chain),

Monet Jewelry and Kimberly Knits, and wanted to get into mail order, which they thought was going to be the distribution system of the future. When General Mills executives made their initial pitch to Eddie Bauer, Niemi's reaction was, "We were doing our own thing and didn't need them. We had not developed our game plan fully and had some basic maturing to do first."

General Mills's Chief Executive Officer James MacFarlane and his immediate prede-cessor, General Ed Rawlins, were both avid outdoorsmen and longtime, devoted Eddie Bauer customers. Rawlins had a son on Mercer Island,

Eddie Bauer to merge with General Mills

By BOYD BURCHARD

Board agreement in princi-ple to merge Seattle's Eddie Bauer, Inc., into General Mills, Inc., Minneapolis, has been announced by James P. McFarland, General Mills board chairman, and Wil-liam F. Niemi, Jr., president of the closely held Seattle-based outdoor-clothing and equipment firm.

Merger completion is sub-ject to submission of a final contract agreement to both boards and to Eddie Bauer, Inc., shareholders for ap-proval. Proposed terms of the year-end common-stock pooling were not disclosed.

Eddie Bauer, Inc., 1737 Airport Way S., is engaged principally in manufacture mail-order

Its Seattle retail outlet is the Eddie Bauer Expedition Outfitter, 1926 Third Ave.

The internationally known Seattle firm had total 1970 sales of about $9 million. General Mills' most recent 12-month sales in its various food, fashion wear, special-ty-chemical and craft-game-toy lines totaled about $1 bil-lion.

The 250-employe Seattle operation, with its 125-em-ploye subsidiary plant in We-tumpka, Ala., is to be oper-ated under its own identity by present officers and staff

as a wholly owned subsidi-ary of General Mills.

Growth of Bauer sales has been "dramatic" in the past 2½ years, Niemi said here. The Seattle retail outlet alone has chalked up sales of over $900,000 since its open-ing last March.

Merger into the giant Gen-eral Mills will permit planned expansion, including establishment of retail out-lets in other major centers of the nation, Niemi noted.

(Additional details in Boyd Burchard's column, D 4.)

and was a frequent visitor at the Eddie Bauer store and offices whenever he came through town. "Rawlins said that they were committed to the specialty retailing business, and if Bauer ever had an interest in joining up with somebody, they would be very interested," recalled Wherry. After coming close to accepting an offer from Quaker Oats, the Bauer team decided that they would be better off with General Mills. "We figured that if we couldn't own the total ship, maybe we could steer it," continued Wherry. "When we couldn't go public, we felt that the best alternative was to join General Mills. One of the most important factors in our decision was that we felt strongly that Betty Crocker stood for the same standard of quality and service that we did."

On March 8, 1971, General Mills acquired Eddie Bauer, Inc., in exchange for 310,736 shares of General Mills common stock. Niemi continued as Eddie Bauer president and was made a vice president of General Mills.

"General Mills's objective was to have Bauer grow as quickly as it could," said Niemi. "The merger took away any of the worry about where the money was going to come from or what our balance sheet looked like. It was certainly exciting to be able to execute these plans in a dramatic manner and see what we could do in terms of expanding product lines and acquiring new mail order customers."

At the time of the acquisition, Eddie Bauer had a national mailing list of about 600,000 names and sent out a total of 2.5 million catalogs a year. To attract more customers, the company bought mailing lists from other catalogs and advertised in specialty publications such as *Outdoor Life*, *Field & Stream* and *American Rifleman*. "We didn't have the name recognition to advertise in general magazines such as Life or Time," recalled Niemi.

New retail stores would bring about greater customer awareness because the company would advertise in local newspapers. The stores would also serve as an extension of the catalog, "which [in turn] was the best communication piece we had to drive traffic into the stores," said Wherry.

Because Bauer's emphasis was on cold-weather products, store sites were selected in northern climates where Bauer already had a critical mass of existing mail order customers and broad name recognition. The second store was built in 1972 in San Francisco, followed by stores in Minneapolis, Denver, Toronto, Chicago and Washington, D.C. (The nation's capitol was the sole exception to the northern-climate strategy.) All the stores were located in healthy downtown areas because, at that time, shopping malls were not as important as they are today. As successful as the stores were, they never cannibalized Bauer's mail order sales, which maintained solid growth in those markets.

Initially, the stores followed the model of the Seattle unit by being the complete apparel and hard goods supplier for hunting, fishing, backpacking, camping and climbing. Like the Seattle store, each new unit featured on-site gunsmiths and fishing tack-

le experts. "Customers would be able to leave the store with everything they needed for their personal expedition, wherever it might be and however long they might be gone," said Bob Murphy, who helped open the first 14 stores after the Seattle unit. The stores sponsored clinics and demonstrations for activities such as snowshoeing, cross-country skiing, avalanche safety, wilderness weather forecasting and duck calling.

In 1973, the company moved its corporate headquarters to a 14-acre campus in Redmond surrounded by abundant stands of alder, hemlock and Douglas fir. It included a wildlife sanctuary for rabbits and quail and a rearing pond for trout.

Despite the peaceful new surroundings, keeping focused on a changing marketplace was tough when considerable effort was expended merging the cultures of the two companies. Eddie Bauer employees who were there at the time remember the respect they had for the General Mills people; it was just that specialty retailing and mail order are far different from supermarket sales. In the first four years under General Mills, Eddie Bauer's sales grew from about $10 million in 1971 to $30 million in 1975, but some knew the growth could have been more dramatic. Also in 1975, Bill Niemi, Jr., who was the last direct thread to the Bauer heritage, resigned to go into business for himself.

Over the next 13 years, the company had a number of chief executive officers. One of them was James J. Casey, a longtime General Mills executive, who was named president of Eddie Bauer in January 1978.

He had been with the company for three years as vice president of finance and controller. During Casey's tenure, General Mills invested in more sophisticated systems, such as a 24-hour toll-free telephone number and computer systems that gave instantaneous and constantly updated inventory-status reports, information on customer demographics and targeted mailing lists based on previous buying patterns.

CHANGING CUSTOMER DEMOGRAPHICS

In the late 1970s and early 1980s, much of the change at Eddie Bauer was driven by the fact that the customers were getting older and had different priorities. Instead of hiking into the woods or going on a hunting or fishing trip for a week or two at a time, they were more interested in a day hike or a weekend camp outing with their family. (The company helped promote family camping activities with a series of guidebooks written by Eddie Bauer and Seattle author Archie Satterfield.)

The company still maintained its utilitarian approach to its apparel. High-quality Bauer goose down was inspected and analyzed in the company's own testing laboratories for composition, loft, resiliency and cleanliness as carefully in those days as it is today. "We always start from the premise that a garment is functional, regardless of end-use," Bob Murphy told the men's wear trade newspaper *Daily News Record* in 1988, when he was in charge of Bauer's outerwear business. "Every piece is con-

structed as if it might be worn mountain climbing. We religiously stick to that premise. Waterproof and breathable functional characteristics are as important to a guy walking his dog as they are to a guy climbing a mountain."

To become a year-round outfitter (rather than just for fall and winter), Bauer intro-

In 1970, faced with a need to raise capital, the company decided to make an initial public offering of stock. When the stock market took a downturn, the offering was postponed.

PRELIMINARY PROSPECTUS DATED MARCH 26, 1970

PROSPECTUS

250,000 Shares
Eddie Bauer, Inc.
Common Stock

THESE SECURITIES HAVE NOT BEEN APPROVED OR DISAPPROVED BY THE SECURITIES AND EXCHANGE COMMISSION NOR HAS THE COMMISSION PASSED UPON THE ACCURACY OR ADEQUACY OF THIS PROSPECTUS. ANY REPRESENTATION TO THE CONTRARY IS A CRIMINAL OFFENSE.

Of the 250,000 shares offered hereby, 62,500 shares are to be sold by the Company and 187,500 shares are to be sold by the stockholders named herein under "Principal and Selling Stockholders." The Company will receive no part of the proceeds from the sale of shares by the Selling Stockholders.

Prior to this offering there has been no public market for the Company's common stock. Accordingly, the public offering price has been determined by negotiation among the Company, the Selling Stockholders and the Underwriters.

	Price to Public	Underwriting Discounts and Commissions	Proceeds to Company[1]	Proceeds to Selling Stockholders[1]
Per Share				
Total				

[1]Before deducting expenses estimated at $ payable by the Company and $ payable by the Selling Stockholders.

These shares are offered by the Underwriters named herein subject to delivery to and acceptance by them and subject to prior sale and to the approval of certain legal matters by counsel. It is expected that delivery of stock certificates will be made on or about   , 1970 at the office of Smith, Barney & Co. Incorporated, 20 Broad Street, New York, N.Y. 10005.

Smith, Barney & Co.
Incorporated

, 1970

A registration statement relating to these securities has been filed with the Securities and Exchange Commission but has not yet become effective. Information contained herein is subject to completion or amendment. These securities may not be sold nor may offers to buy be accepted prior to the time the registration statement becomes effective. This Prospectus shall not constitute an offer to sell or the solicitation of an offer to buy nor shall there be any sale of these securities in any State in which such offer, solicitation or sale would be unlawful prior to registration or qualification under the securities laws of any such State.

THE LATER YEARS OF EDDIE AND STINE

*A*fter his retirement in 1968, Ed and Stine devoted most of their time to their first loves: camping, hunting, fishing and traveling. Every summer they vacationed at their cabin near Neah Bay, on the very northwest tip of Washington State, where the Strait of Juan de Fuca meets the Pacific Ocean. He continued to raise champion Labrador retrievers at his home in the Seattle suburb of Bellevue and wrote a series of guidebooks with author Archie Satterfield, which the company marketed to help promote family camping activities.

Unfortunately, Ed had a bittersweet relationship with the company he created. "We tried desperately to get Ed back," recalled Ken Wherry. "But he refused to even set foot in the [corporate office] building, and never did, although Stine did. Ed sometimes sat in his Cadillac out in the visitors' parking area and we would talk."

John Kime noted that, through all the management changes, "Every once in a while we got a young marketing tiger in here who had gone to the Wharton School of Business and had this wonderful idea he thought nobody else had ever thought of: 'All we have to do is invite Ed to the opening of the new store,' he'd say. Ed wouldn't do that. He was very proud of the fact that he didn't have to depend on any outside source of income."

In 1983, after he was featured in a

cover story in *Pacific Northwest* magazine, Ed agreed to sit for a picture for that winter's Eddie Bauer catalog. "It took a lot of us to try to convince him that it was a good thing to do, but it was one of the most terrific pictures of Ed that we've ever published," Wherry recalled.

Ed died at the age of 86 on April 18, 1986, at Overlake Hospital in Bellevue, Washington — two weeks after Stine, to whom he was married for 56 years, died of pancreatic cancer. Though the official cause of death was cardiac arrest, Eddie C. Bauer felt his father died of a broken heart. "I think he was so depressed — it hit him

Ed and Stine Bauer in the early eighties. Through a life filled with many challenges, victories and even a few defeats, they had tremendous respect for each other. Ed was so saddened by Stine's death that many believe he died of a broken heart.

so hard — that he couldn't go on. He was shaking so bad that...we took him down to Overlake Hospital. Then he went real quick. He lasted two days there." Ed was survived by Eddie C. and three grandchildren.

Ed's was quite a life. A hunter, fisherman and trapper, he will be remembered as a clever inventor, a holder of many patents and a determined entrepreneur who turned his hobbies into his business and managed to parlay a meager cash start of $25 into a multimillion-dollar company. "From age 13 through 68, business was also my hobby," he once said. "It was like one long vacation. I was outdoors most of the time on long wilderness trips, big-game hunting and fishing. I loved every minute of it."

Today, Ed and Stine live on in the life of the Eddie Bauer company, which presents quarterly "Eddie" and "Stine" awards for employees who consistently give the type of outstanding customer service that Eddie believed in so strongly all his life.

duced a line of ultralight spring and summer products, such as nylon/leather hiking boots, polypropylene underwear, insulated jackets, and apparel and footwear for running, exercise, aerobics and biking. As the demand slackened for backpacks and tents for camping, and ropes and pitons for climbing, the hardware mix began to emphasize daypacks and travel packs, as well as sunglasses and gift items such as flashlights and knives.

To accommodate customers' non-sports needs, Bauer increased its stock of stylish, natural-fiber street sportswear — such as chamois cloth shirts, cotton turtlenecks, polo shirts — made by Eddie Bauer as well as recognized brands such as Pendleton and Harris Tweed.

While the product mix was changing, Bauer was expanding. Between 1981 and 1983, the number of stores more than doubled to 27, including the first warm-weather California locations. These new stores reflected a change in retail strategy from an emphasis on large downtown stores to 7,000-square-foot stores in upscale malls, which left no room for less-profitable tents, sleeping bags, fishing rods and guns. Eliminating those items diluted the authentic Bauer outdoors image but the company's objective was to provide what the customers wanted; items that didn't sell simply couldn't be stocked. Eventually all the gun departments were eliminated, but fishing tackle remained for a while in the big downtown stores in Seattle, San Francisco, Minneapolis, Chicago, Toronto and Boston.

The authentic gear lasted as long as it did

"more out of the emotional attachment that the Niemis had to hunting than any good bottom-line reasons," said Wherry. "After we went through trying to cover the losses that we were taking in those areas, it got to the point where it didn't make any sense. But it took us a long time to detach ourselves from that phase of the business." The change was symbolic as well as financial. "The outdoor gear and equipment was the sizzle in the Eddie Bauer presentation," Wherry noted. "However, to this day, we have never lost sight of the fact that our heritage is a key element that differentiates us from everyone else."

On February 1979, the company moved its flagship store to Fifth Avenue and Union Street from the location on Third Avenue and Virginia Street where it had been since 1970. Designed as an integral part of the Rainier Square retail development, the store occupied 30,000 square feet of space in the Skinner Building, including a selling floor with 19,000 square feet. The new location was around the corner from the Washington Athletic Club Building, the site of Ed's sporting goods store in 1938, and a block away from where the Bauer family lived in 1890.

Michael Rayden, who was brought in as Bauer's chief executive officer in 1984, eliminated product categories like camping tents that took up a lot of space and didn't return sufficient dollars per square foot. He also shut down all of Bauer's sewing operations. Prior to joining Bauer, Rayden was a senior vice president of sportswear at Liz Claiborne, Inc., and, before that, head of

merchandising of women's apparel and accessories at F&R Lazarus Co., a division of Federated Department Stores, Inc. With that background, he continued the emphasis on fashionable women's wear and men's wear.

Three years later, Rayden was succeeded by Wayne Badovinus, the first native Washingtonian to head Bauer since Bill Niemi, Jr. Badovinus was a graduate of Moses Lake High School who liked hunting, fishing and camping. He was also a very experienced retailer, having been a top executive with Nordstrom, Carter Hawley Hale Stores, Inc., Frederick & Nelson and Williams-Sonoma, the San Francisco-based kitchen specialty store and catalog company.

A few months after Badovinus's arrival, General Mills, which was going through its own internal identity crisis, decided to divest itself of all operations not related to food processing or food marketing. Eddie Bauer was put on the selling block. (At around the same time, General Mills sold Talbots to the Jusco Co. Ltd. of Japan for $325 million.) It didn't take long for a famous buyer to emerge, a buyer that would enable Eddie Bauer to build a foundation and a vision to take the company into the twenty-first century.

Eddie Bauer merchandise is made to last a long time. This teddy bear was made from the remains of an oft-worn denim skirt by a loyal customer named Donna Nothe Choiniere, who sent her creation and a letter of explanation to the "Dear Folks at Eddie Bauer," which said, "I made a bear for the couch, to hug, and one for you." At right, an Eddie Bauer down-filled comforter.

A New Owner, A New Future

In May 1988, Eddie Bauer entered a new era when it was acquired by Spiegel, Inc., the giant mail order company, which paid General Mills about $260 million in cash. John J. "Jack" Shea, president of Spiegel, called the Bauer acquisition "a very significant step in Spiegel's growth" because it created "excellent synergies." Bauer provided Spiegel, which was a predominantly women's wear company, with an entree into the men's wear business. Shea, who fully appreciated Bauer's unique

market niche and well-developed point of view, told the *Daily News Record* that Bauer would remain an independent operation based in Seattle. "I think it would be suicidal to move them out of there. It's an outdoor catalog and Seattle is an outdoor environment."

It was obvious from the start that Spiegel and Bauer were an ideal fit. Spiegel, which was founded in 1865, boasted one of the industry's most sophisticated mail order systems, particularly in the areas of identifying

new customers and compiling demographic data about current customers. Spiegel annually mailed out 30 million catalogs to what Shea described as "the best customer list in America."

"It wasn't until we joined Spiegel that we had a parent company that fully understood our potential and opportunity and was willing to give us the financial support," said Senior Vice President Ken Wherry. Spiegel greatly accelerated the Eddie Bauer expansion program that began under

General Mills. At the time it was acquired by Spiegel, Bauer had annual sales of $250 million and 58 retail stores in 14 states; by the end of 1993, Bauer reached $1 billion in sales, 294 stores and a catalog business that doubled in volume. "Considering that in 1968–69 we did $5 million, and we didn't do our first $100 million until 1983, you can see the difference in our performance when we were in an alliance with people who truly understood what the opportunity was," said Wherry.

NEW STORE CONCEPTS

Part of that expansion came from greater emphasis on two merchandising areas that had barely reached their potential: women's careerwear, special occasion apparel and accessories; and home furnishings.

Although Bauer had carried women's wear (created by in-house Bauer designers) for many years, it wasn't until 1987 that the company formed a separate women's wear design staff for less-casual apparel. This new women's wear emphasis led to the creation of a separate catalog and retail store operation under the name All Week Long, whose target customer was a sophisticated working woman with a preference for updated, classic pants, shorts, jumpers, skirts, dresses, blouses, sweaters and outerwear.

The company has the ability to expand into other merchandising areas, such as home furnishings, because "the Eddie Bauer name is now recognized as a brand, much like Ralph Lauren and Polo, Liz

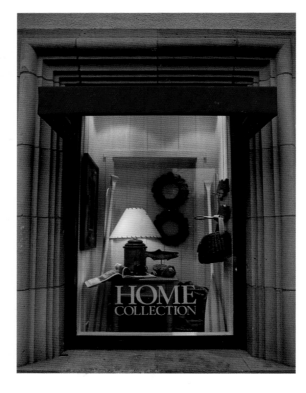

For many years, Eddie Bauer had offered customers home-furnishing items; the Home Division, started in 1991, greatly expanded the breadth of merchandise that reflects the Eddie Bauer tradition. The photo, left, is of a Kansas City Home Collection store; below is the store in the Tacoma Mall.

These pictures from the Oakbrook Center "Premier" Eddie Bauer store in suburban Chicago showcase the best of merchandising. The Eddie Bauer Sport Shop, women's wear and Home Collection are seen in these views.

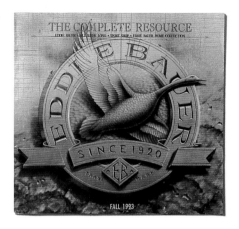

In the early 1990s, the company responded to customer requests and created the Eddie Bauer Sport Shop, a special space within larger Eddie Bauer stores which stocks fly rods, reels and other authentic gear. In September 1993, Eddie Bauer issued "The Complete Resource" catalog, above, which was the company's first perfect-bound catalog. It contained the best of everything Bauer makes.

Claiborne and Levi Strauss. It says 'quality, value, service and style,' which are the very elements that Eddie built this company on," said Richard T. "Rick" Fersch, who was named president in 1993. "We have a strong, visionary product development team that drives our company. We can open 50 stores a year, but we have to have the right product to be able to drive that."

In 1991, the company created a new Home Division, which was inspired by — and built upon — the credibility of the Eddie Bauer authentic outdoor lifestyle. For many years, Bauer offered customers items such as goose-down comforters and pillows, flannel sheets and a variety of bedding and bath items. But with the establishment of the Home Division, offerings expanded to hardwood dining tables and chairs; uphol-stered sofas, chairs and beds; bed frames, tabletop, domestics, bath, kitchen, garden and lighting, as well as novelty items, including compost bins, fire-place tools and mailboxes. By the end of 1994, there were 15 Eddie Bauer Home Stores in 11 states, and separate Home catalogs that are mailed out six times a year.

In the early 1990s, when so many apparel stores in shopping malls were stocking the same basic items and colors in order to emulate the highly successful Gap stores, Eddie Bauer

needed to find a way to distinguish itself from the competition. At the same time, long-term Eddie Bauer customers were requesting the authentic outdoor gear for which the company has always been famous. The company responded by going back to its roots, installing a new concept called the Eddie Bauer Sport Shop — a small (800-square-foot) space in larger Eddie Bauer stores — stocked with fly rods and reels, and authentic hats, apparel, boots, leather goods and other items crafted as an updated reflection of the Eddie Bauer heritage. Bauer also reintroduced several new family camping products, including a lightweight (under 30 pounds) six-person tent and goose-down-insulated sleeping bags.

The Sport Shop was combined with Eddie Bauer Sportswear, All Week Long and the Home Collection under a retail merchandising concept called the "Premier" Eddie Bauer store, which opened in 1991 at the Oakbrook Center in suburban Chicago. Each section of the store is distinguished by its physical layout and decor. The Premier stores proved to be a great success — the volume generated from one Premier store equaled that of five smaller Eddie Bauer stores. In 1993, another Premier store was added in Kansas City at Country Club Plaza.

DEEDEE JONROWE

One of the best examples of Eddie Bauer's renewed commitment to authentic outdoor gear has been the Product Development staff's custom-designed, high-tech racing suits for veteran sled-dog musher, DeeDee Jonrowe, who has raced under Eddie Bauer sponsorship since 1990. Each year, Eddie Bauer outfits the resident of Willow, Alaska, with new racing clothes (from the skin out), gear for her sled and some 7,000 booties to keep ice from collecting on the feet of her 20 dogs.

Ever since 1980, Jonrowe has participated in many races, most notably Alaska's famed Iditarod Trail Sled Dog Race. Known as "The Last Great Race on Earth," the Iditarod is a grueling 1,049-mile trek, starting in downtown Anchorage and running through dense forests, over jagged mountain ranges, down the frozen Yukon River, across desolate tundra and along the wind-blown Arctic coastline to Nome.

The Iditarod Trail, which has become a national historic trail, was originally a mail and supply route from the coastal towns of Seward and Knik to the interior mining camps to the west coast communities, culminating at Nome. (Iditarod means distant place in the Ingalik and Holikachuk Alaskan

native languages.)

In 1993, Jonrowe placed second in the Iditarod, setting a new women's speed record of 10 days, 16 hours, 10 minutes and 50 seconds. That year she was voted "Most Inspirational Musher" by her fellow competitors for courage and perseverance in the face of trail adversity.

In 1994, she arrived in Nome in ninth place, marking her seventh consecutive top-ten finish. Her time was 11 days, four hours, 25 minutes, 15 seconds.

After each race, Jonrowe gives Eddie Bauer engineers valuable information about the effectiveness of her race clothing and gear (which are made by the company's Special Orders department) so that they can make improvements on both her outfits and on items developed for Eddie Bauer customers.

Jonrowe consistently wins awards for the expert handling of her dogs, including "Best-Cared-For Team" in the 1992 Alpirod (through the Alps of France, Austria, Switzerland and Italy), the Leonhard Seppala Humanitarian Award, voted on by the race veterinarians in the 1991 Iditarod, and the "Dog's Best Friend" in the 1989 Kuskokwim 300, which is run in Alaska.

DeeDee Jonrowe, one of the world's greatest sled dog mushers, competes in a racing suit made for her by Eddie Bauer. DeeDee is pictured in action in the Alaskan Iditarod.

On the mail order side of the business, the four concepts — Eddie Bauer Sportswear, All Week Long, Home and the Eddie Bauer Sport Shop — were grouped together for the first time in September 1993 in "The Complete Resource," the company's first catalog that represented all business concepts.

Another example is the "Eddie Bauer Edition" vehicles that have been manufactured since 1983 by the Ford Motor Company. The line started with the Eddie Bauer Bronco II off-road vehicle and now includes the best-selling Explorer and full-size Bronco. The F-Series pickup was unveiled in 1994 to commemorate the 10th anniversary of the Ford/Bauer relationship.

The Ford Motor Company has been manufacturing Eddie Bauer edition vehicles since 1983. Some Eddie Bauer stores, such as the one in Kansas City, have placed Explorer vehicles on display as a means of promoting the long-term relationship.

While other designer-named vehicles have come and gone, this partnership, based on quality and value with an outdoor heritage, continues to be successful. There are more than 500,000 Eddie Bauer Edition vehicles on the road today.

SALES ASSOCIATES

Eddie Bauer's most important assets are thousands of associates whose spirit and dedication maintain and nourish the legend of Eddie Bauer. As Eddie Bauer grows, it becomes increasingly important to find ways to keep the company "small" in spirit and maintain a family feeling that transcends job, department and region.

This is done in a variety of ways. When first joining the company, new associates view a training video that portrays Ed's life and accomplishments, highlights his creed and guarantee and details the company's metamorphosis since it was acquired by Spiegel, Inc. All associates receive *Toongabbie*, the in-house publication, which is full of the latest company news — including special events and sightings of celebrity shoppers — as well as valuable tips on how to give better customer service.

To help promote camaraderie, the company counts on the ideas of dedicated associates who volunteer to serve on the Bauer Arts and Recreation Committee (BARC) which plans, coordinates and publicizes a wide assortment of group social activities, from Seattle Mariners' baseball games to scuba diving classes. These activities are capped off with a magnificent company-sponsored picnic for more than 2,000 associates, friends and family, who

enjoy outstanding entertainment and get to participate in a variety of sporting events. Associates who work outside of Seattle are allocated funds to create their own social events at the discretion of the regional managers.

Every quarter, Eddie Bauer publicity honors associates' contributions to sales, profit or customer satisfaction with one of three different Legend Awards: The Stine Award, which represents an exceptional achievement *within* an associate's current responsibilities; the Eddie Award, which recognizes an extraordinary individual accomplishment *beyond* an associate's job

description; and the Bauer Award, which honors exceptional team efforts *outside* team members' normal responsibilities. The winners are publicized in the *Toongabbie* and are given a plaque and cash awards, an invitation to the quarterly Legend Award luncheon and recognition on the Legend Award board.

Bauer's highest honors are represented by the "Best of Bauer" awards, which are given to sales-support (non-sales) associates who have demonstrated exemplary customer service, contributed to outstanding sales and profits or originated creative ideas. In the store division, selection is based on the highest annual comparable sales increase over the previous year. Awards are given to the top regional manager, the top eight district managers and the top 40 store managers.

Employee communications is an important part of the Eddie Bauer culture, as are training programs, incentive awards and company gatherings that promote camaraderie. *Toongabbie* is an informative magazine that keeps all associates abreast of company news.

Associates learn they are winners with a creative flourish, such as a balloon bouquet. A proclamation is also presented. Winners are invited to attend the "Best of Bauer" conference, which is the most visible and highly acclaimed program in the company. These conferences are part of an all-expenses-paid trip to a resort, where associates set aside time to participate in Think Tanks — brainstorming sessions on key corporate topics that often are incorporated into the company's goals and objectives for the following year. Sales associates who are part of the winning store teams are honored at a special "Best of Bauer" event in their area.

Eddie Bauer believes that successful companies must make the extra effort to nourish the minds and bodies of its associates. Eddie Bauer University is a resource base of training options and information, offering a variety of on-site classes, from the latest word processing software to the data processing systems. The Employee Assistance Program offers outsourcing programs and information on dieting, stress management, alcohol and chemical dependencies, prenatal care, elder care and child care and other concerns. Bauer also offers the Outdoor Experience Allowance. Under this program, the company provides associates a stipend for lessons in sports that they have never tried before.

By participating in outdoor activities — such as snow sports, water sports, mountaineering/biking, fishing and scuba diving — associates attain a greater appreciation for Eddie Bauer's heritage and culture.

RETAIL'S BRAVE NEW WORLD

The brave new world of retail — both stores and catalogs — has never been more complicated than it is in the 1990s. To lead Eddie Bauer, Spiegel selected Rick Fersch, who replaced Alton Withers, Spiegel's executive vice president and chief executive officer. (Withers held those posts for about a year on an interim basis after Wayne Badovinus resigned in 1992, four years after Spiegel bought the company.) Fersch, who had been in retail for more than two decades, worked for Eddie Bauer for six years as vice president of stores (as well as

The Eddie Bauer flagship store in downtown Seattle is around the corner from the Washington Athletic Club where Ed moved his business in 1938. The Daruma, an eyeless Japanese doll, has its eyes painted in as a project progresses. This one was part of a ceremony initiating the first Eddie Bauer stores in Japan.

CORPORATE CITIZENSHIP

Corporate citizenship, community involvement and promotion of environmental issues further exemplify the Eddie Bauer spirit. The company compensates associates for eight hours of volunteer work on community projects that are coordinated through their local Easter Seals or United Way chapter. In turn, associates contribute a matching eight hours on their own time. One example of the handiwork of Bauer associates can be seen at the Easter Seals Gig Harbor (Washington) camp, where Bauer volunteers rebuilt the dock, float and trails, and persuaded one of the company's vendors to build a new sign. (Easter Seals is a preferred charity because its camps across the country provide accessibility to the out-of-doors for disabled people.)

The company has long been a corporate sponsor for Ducks Unlimited, a non-profit national organization concerned with the preservation of wetlands in the Canadian breeding grounds where 8 percent of all ducks are hatched. This activity recalls the young Eddie Bauer's caring for wild Chinese pheasant hens for their protection and propagation, about which he felt it "was my duty to always put back more than I took."

The tradition of helping others is a continuing part of the legacy of Eddie Bauer.

executive vice president for merchandising, marketing and advertising and chief operating officer).

The fall 1994 Resource catalog introduced A.K.A. Eddie Bauer, a line of finely crafted clothing for men and women; the collection has a finished sportswear look for times when Eddie Bauer Sportswear is too casual. That same season saw the opening of the first three retail stores in Tokyo, Japan, where Bauer products had been sold for many years in other stores under the "Eddie Bauer" label and where the company had traditionally done a large mail order business. Eddie Bauer has also extended its international reach with inserts featuring Eddie Bauer products in Otto Versand's Sport-Scheck catalogs, which are distributed throughout Germany.

Also in 1994, Spiegel and Time Warner Entertainment joined together to launch two new home shopping channels for cable television to sell merchandise for the family and the home. The first, called "Catalog 1," was a 24-hour "video mall" service offering fashion accessories, children's products and home furnishings from several different catalog companies, including Spiegel and Eddie Bauer, Neiman Marcus, Crate & Barrel, Williams-Sonoma, The Sharper Image, The Nature Company and Time Warner's Viewer's Edge. The second channel, testing on Time Warner's cable system in Orlando, Florida, will be fully interactive, enabling consumers to use a special remote control device to "enter" any catalog store at any time, view merchandise in full-motion video and make purchases.

As exciting as the future looks, and as many changes as it will bring, the Eddie Bauer way of doing business — whether face-to-face with the customer, over telephone lines or via fiber-optic cable — remains the same. Although the product line has transformed radically, "the concept that Eddie initiated is the concept that we continue to build on today," said Fersch. "Some people say if we're not selling tents, we're not true to Eddie Bauer. I don't think Eddie Bauer ever said 'tents are my business.' He was a practical man. If the customer wanted a shuttlecock, then he sold a shuttlecock. If a high-quality shuttlecock wasn't available, he invented a new, greatly improved one. He focused his time and attention on quality, value and service, and that's what we focus on today. His creed and his guarantee are so good, you'd almost think they were created by a Madison Avenue advertising agency. If you were going to start a company today, you would use as its foundation the principles that Eddie Bauer stood for. The important thing for our company is to interpret Eddie's way of doing business to the customer of the nineties and beyond."

THE EDDIE BAUER SPIRIT

Through all the company's changes, from a small leased space at Bob Newton's Gun Shop to a billion-dollar international corporation, "The Eddie Bauer spirit is the single most significant thing that has kept us together," said Ken Wherry. "Through our ups and downs, we have maintained our commitment to the customer in both quality and service. Ed felt very strongly that to earn anybody's high esteem, you had to provide beyond their expectations the service, value and quality that they were looking for. That is the rope — not the thread — that has kept the whole thing together."

"As big and as complex as the company has gotten," said Rick Fersch, "and as much change as there's been, Eddie Bauer still attracts a certain type of person that likes the small, family, team approach to doing things. You become a part of something bigger than yourself and you can really accomplish wonderful things," whether helping to design and market a new item or creating and opening a new store concept.

It is only fitting that the final words to this story belong to Eddie himself, because they are just as relevant today for a billion-dollar international firm as they were when he first opened the doors of Bauer's Sport Shop on Seneca Street.

"During my 55 years of outfitting, I watched many outfitters grow and prosper, then close their doors because they failed to keep up with the ever-changing needs and wants of their customers. My business grew and prospered because I never failed to lead in creating new and better products and in providing better services...that made our company what it is today."

CALENDAR OF SIGNIFICANT EVENTS

1899
Eddie Bauer was born on Orcas Island, on October 19.

1913
Eddie Bauer got his first job in sporting goods, with Piper & Taft.

1919
Ed won a national contest for speed and proficiency in stringing tournament-caliber tennis rackets.

1920
Ed opened Eddie Bauer's Tennis Shop.

1929
Eddie Bauer and Christine "Stine" Heltborg were married on February 21.

1934
Ed secured U.S. and Canadian patents on a badminton shuttlecock.

1935
Ed introduced the patented Blizzard-Proof® jacket, a quilted garment filled with goose down. (It was later improved and renamed the Skyliner®.)

1938
Ed moved retail operations to a store on Union Street and Fifth Avenue, in the Washington Athletic Club Building, in Seattle.

1942
Ed launched the Eddie Bauer Expedition Outfitters mail-order division, selling goose-down garments and goose-down-insulated sleeping bags.

1942
Ed began producing garments and sleeping bags in support of the war effort.

1945
Eddie Bauer Expedition Outfitters sent out its first mail-order catalog.

1948
William F. Niemi, Sr., joined Eddie Bauer, Inc.

1949
The company was renamed the William F. Niemi Co., doing business as Eddie Bauer Expedition Outfitters.

1951
Eddie Bauer officially abandoned the retail store business when the inventory and accounts receivable of the store were sold to Frederick & Nelson, the Seattle department store.

1953
The original William F. Niemi Co. was dissolved and a new William F. Niemi Co. was formed as a fifty-fifty partnership between Eddie Bauer and William F. Niemi, Sr. The partners set up a sewing/manufacturing operation on South Jackson Street.

1953
Eddie Bauer outfitted an expedition to scale 28,250-foot Mount Godwin Austen (K-2), then the world's highest unconquered peak.

1961
Manufacturing and mail-order operations were moved to 417 East Pine Street and Summit Avenue.

1963
Eddie Bauer outfitted the successful Mt. Everest expedition, when Jim Whittaker of Seattle became the first American to reach the top of the tallest mountain in the world.

1968
Eddie Bauer and his son, Eddie C. Bauer, sold their interest in the company to William F. Niemi, Sr., and William F. Niemi, Jr. The company was incorporated as Eddie Bauer, Inc., succeeding the William F. Niemi, Inc. partnership.

1968
The company moved to new headquarters on Airport Way.

1970
The new Eddie Bauer regime opened its first large store on Third Avenue & Virginia Street in downtown Seattle.

1971
General Mills, Inc., acquired Eddie Bauer, Inc., on March 8.

1972
Eddie Bauer's second store opened in Minneapolis.

1973
The company moved its corporate headquarters to Redmond.

1974
Ed was named "Retriever Breeder of the Year" by the Professional Retrievers Trainers Association.

1983
Eddie Bauer edition vehicles introduced by the Ford Motor Company.

1986
Ed died at the age of 86 on April 18 — two weeks after the death of Stine, to whom he was married for 56 years.

1979
The company moved its flagship store in February to Fifth Avenue and Union Street.

1988
Eddie Bauer was acquired in May by Spiegel, Inc.

1991
The company launched a new retail merchandising concept called the "Premier" Eddie Bauer store at the Oakbrook Mall in suburban Chicago.

1993
The company mailed out "The Complete Resource," its first perfect-bound mail-order catalog in September.

1993
Spiegel and Eddie Bauer's 1.5 million-square-foot distribution center opened in Groveport, Ohio.

1994
Eddie Bauer opened its first three retail stores in Japan.

1995
Eddie Bauer celebrated its 75th Anniversary.

DIRECTORY OF STORES

The map shows where Eddie Bauer stores can be found as this book goes to press.

From a small shop in the heart of downtown Seattle, Eddie Bauer has diversified and expanded into every strategic retail market in the United States and Canada. Under General Mills's ownership, stores were first opened in San Francisco and Minneapolis in 1972, followed by Chicago and Denver in 1973. The first Canadian location was Toronto in 1974. Expansion accelerated under Spiegel; today there are over 260 Eddie Bauer Sportswear stores, nine All Week Long stores, 17 Home stores and 35 Outlets across the country, with three stores in Tokyo, Japan.

LEGEND

■ Multiple stores in one city or surrounding area

● Single store

ACKNOWLEDGEMENTS

As with any book, many people made valuable contributions to make this one a reality.

Among Eddie Bauer people, thanks and appreciation go to all those who allowed me to record their thoughts and recollections, with special thanks to Susan Connole for her energy and enthusiasm; John Kime for his corporate memory and good humor; Ken Wherry and Bob Murphy for their careful reading of this manuscript; and Marsha Savery for initiating and overseeing the entire project.

Eddie Christian Bauer provided insight on his parents and furnished us with rare photographs. William F. Niemi, Jr., gave us an understanding of the contributions of his father to the Eddie Bauer Company as well as information on how the company operated in the 1960s and 1970s.

Thanks to publisher Mowry Mann for his solid support and keen judgment; Tim Connolly, senior project manager, for his invaluable assistance; and Ceila Robbins for her gentle and meticulous editing.

Finally, my boundless thanks to my wife, Marybeth, and my daughter, Fae.

Robert Spector

Seattle, Washington